# Surrey and Sussex by Rail

A guide to the routes, scenery and towns

# ACKNOWLEDGEMENTS

Every editor relies on the knowledge and expertise of others, and I am grateful to all the various authors who have contributed so willingly to the success of this book. I am indebted to H. Trevor Jones (RDS London Branch Chairman) for his editorial assistance and advice and for sharing the thankless task of word processing the text; to Mr McGill of Westbury for the excellent map and line diagrams; to those RDS members who commented on the text and to those who supplied additional material. I regret being unable to use everything offered. But any mistakes are probably due as much to my additions or amendments as to the original contributors' work.

I must also thank my wife Hazel, without whose help, advice, and tolerance this book would not have appeared.

**Graham Collett,** Bromley, Kent, January 1988

# EDITOR'S NOTES

**Scenic Routes**
The reader is urged to travel the secondary routes for their greater scenic interest. The Editor's own preferred scenic routes are Pulborough–Arundel; Guildford–Reigate; and Edenbridge–Uckfield. But the Brighton–Lewes–Eastbourne–Hastings route is also highly recommended. With a Rail Rover or Runabout ticket, there are plenty of opportunities for scenic round trips. It is also often possible to buy return tickets which enable you to come back by an alternative route.

**Train Services**
All train services (except Dorking–Horsham) referred to in this guide run hourly or more frequently on Mondays to Saturdays. Most routes still have at least an hourly service on Sundays, but trains are liable to delays and diversions when the track is being repaired (also sometimes on Saturdays). You are advised to check times in advance if travelling at week-ends.

**Buses**
Major changes to bus services have taken place over the course of the last eighteen months (and further changes are likely to occur) as a result of bus deregulation. All bus information given here is based on 1987-88 timetables and refers to travel roughly between 9 a.m. and 5 p.m. Mondays to Saturdays, unless otherwise indicated. There are few rural buses in the evening or on Sundays or Public Holidays.

**Railway Terminology**
The UP line or platform is that used by trains travelling towards London; the DOWN line or platform is the opposite.

**Abbreviations**
| | |
|---|---|
| BR | British Rail |
| DMU | Diesel Multiple Unit (diesel train without locomotive) |
| EMU | Electric Multiple Unit (cf. DMU) (the principal type of rolling-stock on the Southern Region of BR) |
| KESR | *Kent and East Sussex by Rail* (a companion guide-book to this volume) |
| LBSCR | London, Brighton & South Coast Railway |
| LSWR | London & South Western Railway |
| RDS | Railway Development Society |
| SER | South Eastern Railway |

Front cover: Arundel Castle (Photo: Peter Smith)
Back cover: Beachy Head
Inside front cover: Brighton Pavilion
Title-page: An EMU, widely used on Southern Region's coastal routes (Photo: British Rail)

# CONTENTS

| | |
|---|---|
| Acknowledgements | 2 |
| Editor's Notes | 2 |
| Area Map | 4 |
| Introduction | 6 |
| 1  London Victoria–Gatwick Airport–Haywards Heath–Brighton by John Barfield and Clive Davies | 7 |
| Brighton by H. Trevor Jones | 11 |
| 2  East Croydon–East Grinstead by Laurence Skinnerton and Graham Collett | 12 |
| The Bluebell Railway by Laurence Skinnerton and Graham Collett | 15 |
| 3  The Wealden Line: Oxted–Edenbridge–Uckfield by John Bigny and A. Raleigh Mordaunt | 16 |
| 4  Tonbridge–Redhill by Mark Bigny | 22 |
| 5  Haywards Heath–Lewes–Seaford by H. Trevor Jones | 24 |
| 6  Brighton–Lewes–Eastbourne–Hastings by H. Trevor Jones | 28 |
| 7  London Victoria–Sutton–Horsham by I. McGill | 32 |
| 8  Gatwick Airport–Chichester (including Littlehampton and Bognor Regis) by Simon A. Jeffs | 36 |
| Arundel by Laurel Arnison and H. Trevor Jones | 40 |
| 9  Brighton–Portsmouth Harbour by Hugh R. Fowler, Mark Hosking, and H. Trevor Jones | 41 |
| Chichester by Mark Hosking and Laurel Arnison | 46 |
| 10 Guildford–Redhill by I. McGill | 47 |
| 11 London Waterloo–Guildford via Cobham by I. McGill | 51 |
| Leatherhead–Effingham Junction by I. McGill | 54 |
| A Walk Round Guildford by Clive Davies, John Barfield, and I. McGill | 54 |
| 12 London Waterloo–Guildford–Portsmouth Harbour by Ken Wright and Mark Hosking | 56 |
| The City of Portsmouth by Ken Wright | 61 |
| Further Information | 62 |
| Select Bibliography | 63 |
| Index | 64 |
| Other books in the *by Rail* series | Inside back cover |

Littlehampton – seen from across the River Arun (Photo: H. Trevor Jones)

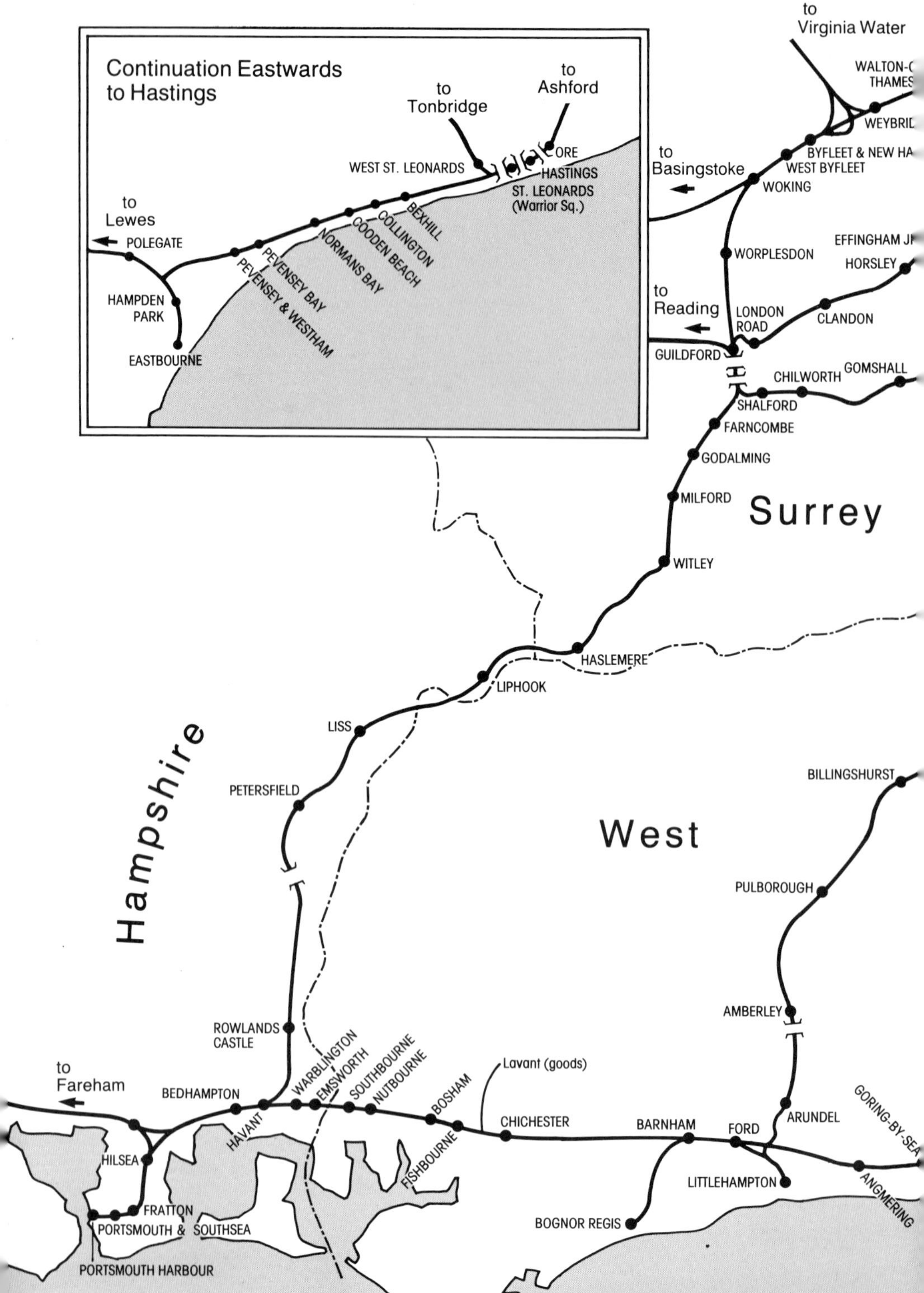

Continuation Eastwards to Hastings
to Tonbridge
to Ashford
ORE
WEST ST. LEONARDS
HASTINGS
ST. LEONARDS (Warrior Sq.)
to Lewes
POLEGATE
BEXHILL
COLLINGTON
COODEN BEACH
NORMANS BAY
PEVENSEY BAY
PEVENSEY & WESTHAM
HAMPDEN PARK
EASTBOURNE
to Virginia Water
WALTON-O
THAMES
WEYBRID
BYFLEET & NEW HA
WEST BYFLEET
to Basingstoke
WOKING
EFFINGHAM JI
HORSLEY
WORPLESDON
to Reading
LONDON ROAD
CLANDON
GUILDFORD
CHILWORTH
GOMSHALL
SHALFORD
FARNCOMBE
GODALMING
MILFORD
Surrey
WITLEY
HASLEMERE
LIPHOOK
LISS
PETERSFIELD
Hampshire
West
BILLINGSHURST
PULBOROUGH
AMBERLEY
ROWLANDS CASTLE
to Fareham
BEDHAMPTON
WARBLINGTON
EMSWORTH
SOUTHBOURNE
NUTBOURNE
BOSHAM
Lavant (goods)
CHICHESTER
BARNHAM
FORD
ARUNDEL
GORING-BY-SEA
HAVANT
FISHBOURNE
HILSEA
FRATTON
PORTSMOUTH & SOUTHSEA
PORTSMOUTH HARBOUR
BOGNOR REGIS
LITTLEHAMPTON
ANGMERING

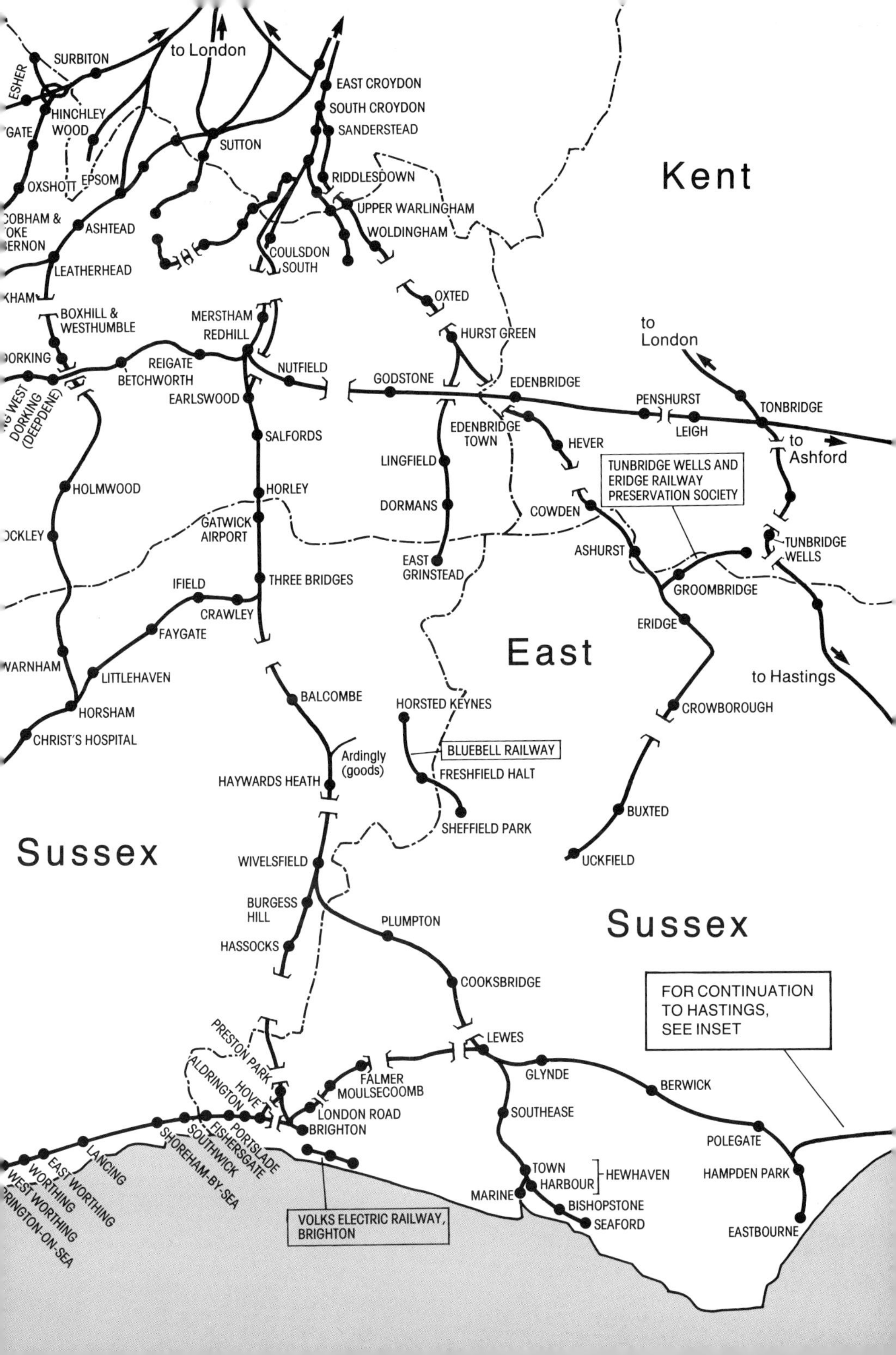
to London
SURBITON
HINCHLEY WOOD
EAST CROYDON
SOUTH CROYDON
SANDERSTEAD
SUTTON
EPSOM
OXSHOTT
RIDDLESDOWN
UPPER WARLINGHAM
WOLDINGHAM
Kent
ASHTEAD
COULSDON SOUTH
LEATHERHEAD
OXTED
BOXHILL & WESTHUMBLE
MERSTHAM
REDHILL
HURST GREEN
to London
REIGATE
NUTFIELD
GODSTONE
EDENBRIDGE
BETCHWORTH
PENSHURST
TONBRIDGE
EARLSWOOD
EDENBRIDGE TOWN
LEIGH
to Ashford
DORKING (DEEPDENE)
SALFORDS
HEVER
TUNBRIDGE WELLS AND ERIDGE RAILWAY PRESERVATION SOCIETY
LINGFIELD
HOLMWOOD
HORLEY
DORMANS
COWDEN
GATWICK AIRPORT
ASHURST
TUNBRIDGE WELLS
EAST GRINSTEAD
THREE BRIDGES
GROOMBRIDGE
IFIELD
CRAWLEY
ERIDGE
FAYGATE
East
LITTLEHAVEN
to Hastings
HORSHAM
BALCOMBE
HORSTED KEYNES
CROWBOROUGH
CHRIST'S HOSPITAL
BLUEBELL RAILWAY
Ardingly (goods)
HAYWARDS HEATH
FRESHFIELD HALT
BUXTED
SHEFFIELD PARK
Sussex
WIVELSFIELD
UCKFIELD
BURGESS HILL
PLUMPTON
Sussex
HASSOCKS
COOKSBRIDGE
FOR CONTINUATION TO HASTINGS, SEE INSET
PRESTON PARK
LEWES
FALMER
MOULSECOOMB
GLYNDE
BERWICK
HOVE
ALDRINGTON
LONDON ROAD
BRIGHTON
SOUTHEASE
PORTSLADE
FISHERSGATE
SOUTHWICK
SHOREHAM-BY-SEA
LANCING
EAST WORTHING
WORTHING
WEST WORTHING
POLEGATE
HAMPDEN PARK
TOWN
HARBOUR
HEWHAVEN
MARINE
BISHOPSTONE
SEAFORD
VOLKS ELECTRIC RAILWAY, BRIGHTON
EASTBOURNE

# INTRODUCTION

There are many parts of the country with beautiful scenery and interesting places to visit, and there are many parts with frequent interconnecting train services over a network of routes. The area covered by this guide-book fits both bills. In addition there is also quite a good network of buses, at least during the daytime on weekdays, that fills in the gaps not covered by the rail network.

*Surrey and Sussex by Rail* is one of a series of guide-books compiled by the Railway Development Society, an independent voluntary body serving the interests of all rail-users. In this book we have attempted to show how public transport, especially the railways, can be used to the full in that part of England lying south and south-west of London. The presence of so many regular commuters to London has ensured the survival of a more comprehensive rural rail network in this area than in many other parts of the country. Most places mentioned in the text can be visited for just an hour or two, at any time of day, simply by alighting from one train and continuing on the next or the next-but-one.

This book gives a flavour, line by line, of what you can see from the train as well as what you can visit by alighting from it. It is assumed the reader possesses a current rail timetable, so only generalised references are made to train services. Information about bus routes to places off the railway is also given.

We have written with the general reader in mind, although we have included a few items of specialist interest. We have also mentioned some useful passenger facilities, such as station buffets.

Holmbury St Mary (Photo: I. McGill)

# 1
# LONDON VICTORIA–GATWICK AIRPORT–HAYWARDS HEATH–BRIGHTON
### by John Barfield and Clive Davies

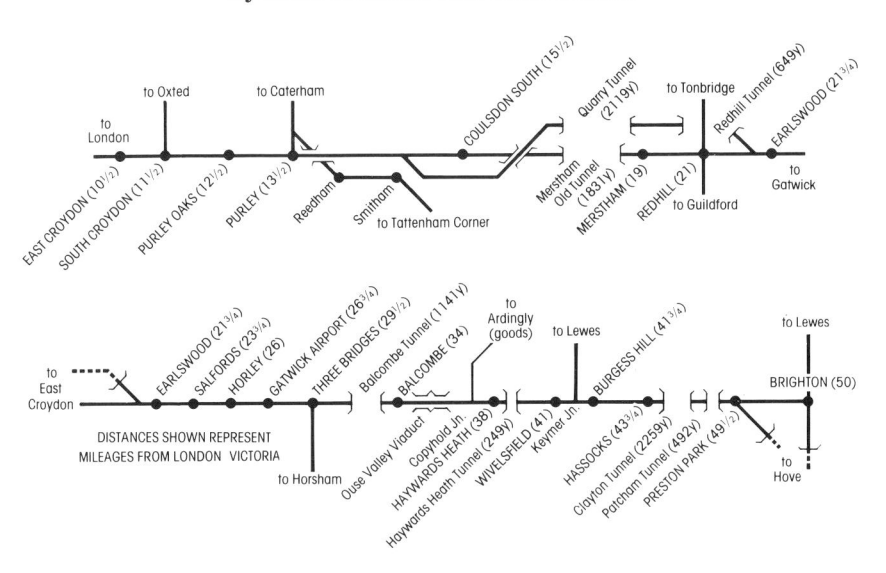

While the original route to Brighton (completed in 1841) started from London Bridge, most travellers to Brighton now depart from the terminus at **Victoria**, first opened by the LBSCR in 1860 and greatly enlarged at the turn of the century. Indeed, it has been immortalised by the film *London to Brighton in 3 Minutes*. Its famous Pullman train the 'Southern Belle' was superseded by a dedicated Pullman EMU set, the 'Brighton Belle' which ran from 1932 to 1972. The present service includes, in addition to the regular hourly fast trains to Brighton, the 'Gatwick Express', a dedicated non-stop service to Gatwick Airport running every fifteen minutes.

Having cleared the Victoria terminus and surmounted the bank, one sees on the right the distinctive tower of the Thames Water Authority pumping-station next to Grosvenor Dock, once the access to a canal which led to the terminus itself. Part of the canal still exists for the Gatliff Road waste transfer depot run by Westminster City Council. Next can be seen the sweep of chains which support Chelsea Bridge and one glimpses for a second the trees of Battersea Park, which formed part of the Festival of Britain complex in 1951, but which is now more famous for its fun-fair and the recently completed Peace Pagoda.

As the Chatham line to Dover veers off to the left between the palatial towers of Battersea power-station (soon to be converted with much of the land around it into a massive leisure complex) and the famous gasholder, the train speeds through **Battersea Park** Station. It then curves sharply to cross over the former LSWR main-line from Waterloo to Bournemouth, and the maze of lines which weave under to connect the South Eastern lines with Stewarts Lane depot and the West London line. Our train then runs parallel with some ten tracks for about a mile to the biggest interchange station on the BR system, with no less than seventeen platforms,

**Clapham Junction**. This station is shortly to receive a much-needed facelift, as part of an adjacent major shopping-centre development.

On the right the campanile tower of the Chelsea Harbour development, Lots Road power-station, and the tower blocks of Worlds End backed by the Empress State Building can be seen, while the ridge to the left is peaked by some of the more grandiose turreted terraces fronting Clapham Common.

While not yet clear of the London suburbs the next few miles are relatively rural as, parting abruptly from the Bournemouth line, the train plunges into a leafy cutting through **Wandsworth Common** and the station of that name; thence to **Balham**, immortalised by Peter Sellers in his famous record as 'Gateway to the South'.

As the lines to Tulse Hill and Crystal Palace branch off to the left, the Crystal Palace and Norwood television transmitters may be glimpsed. We then cross Tooting Bec Common, meeting another complex of lines just before **Streatham Common**, where the strange Oriental building on the left is another water pumping-station. Thence we pass through **Norbury** and **Thornton Heath** to **Selhurst** where one is suddenly confronted, both on the left and right, with another maze of lines and sidings, a veritable Crewe of the Southern. This is Selhurst depot where a large amount of stock is both stored and serviced – some ending its days in ignominious dereliction.

The line to West Croydon curves away sharply to the right, and then the original line from London Bridge comes in from the left. Soon, to the right, the skyscrapers of Croydon come into view as the train pulls into **East Croydon** – the first stop for most trains ('Gatwick Express' apart) – while on the left can be seen the hills of Addington. These provide the first indication that the journey is suddenly to become particularly interesting, as the line reaches the northern outcrop of the North Downs and the first real countryside of the trip.

The line continues in a cutting to **South Croydon**, where the first major divergence, to the left, is that of the line to East Grinstead (described in Chapter 2). Next on our line come **Purley Oaks** followed by **Purley**, where lines dive off in both directions to Caterham and Tattenham Corner.

The train gathers speed as it burrows into the chalk of the North Downs, races over the main Brighton road, and appears to leap-frog over itself before plunging into Quarry Tunnel and emerging to cross the M25, London's outer orbital road. Passing sand and gravel workings to the left it then flings itself into Redhill Tunnel, suddenly emerging at last into open Surrey countryside.

But what, you may ask, has happened to **Redhill**, the junction for the cross-country routes to Tonbridge (Chapter 4) and to Guildford (Chapter 10)? (be warned that trains going in opposite directions may share the same platform at Redhill). Here a bit of history creeps in. The original Redhill Station was built by the SER in 1844. It was rebuilt in 1858, but remained owned and operated by the SER until 1923 – despite the opening of their Sevenoaks Cut-Off (the present Charing Cross mainline) in 1868. This led to many disputes between the LBSCR and the SER over whose trains should have priority. When the growth of traffic led to the widening of the Brighton mainline in the 1890s the LBSCR chose a route that would avoid Redhill, and built a separate pair of tracks from the former Coulsdon North Station (closed comparatively recently) to Earlswood Junction. This is the present route used by Brighton line expresses and is known as the 'Quarry line'.

Just beyond **Earlswood** can be seen, on the left, the square grey tower of the Royal Earlswood Institution. The line continues largely on an embankment through rolling fields to **Salfords**, a not very prepossessing station served only by the slow lines. On a fine clear day, however, there is to the right a splendid view of the southern escarpment of the North Downs towards Dorking and Guildford (described in more detail in Chapter 10).

Very shortly one comes to **Horley** which, with its vast expanse of commuter car

*Left:* RDS members inspect one of the new Class 319 EMUs which will operate from Bedford to Gatwick Airport and Brighton via the reopened 'Thameslink' tunnel (Photo: Graham Collett)
*Right:* Brighton, The Lanes (Photo: H. Atkinson)

parks, indicates that something larger is to come. Indeed one is soon in the ultra-modern **Gatwick Airport** Station, with its six platforms, on the site of the former Gatwick Racecourse Station (closed in 1935 but reopened in 1958 to serve the new airport). Look out for what remains of the original Gatwick Airport Station (also known as Tinsley Green) about a mile farther on.

The station in its recently rebuilt form is an impressive enterprise connected with the airport by a massive space frame concourse and escalators and effectively forming part of it as the facilities extend both sides of the tracks. Note also on the right the 'people mover' similar to the one at Birmingham International. Escalators lead up from the main platforms straight into the airport terminal complex, which serves an extensive network of intercontinental, European, and domestic routes, operated by many airlines. The planes may be watched from a public viewing area on the roof of the terminal; remember to take your ear-plugs! The station book-stall does teas and coffees, but for any substantial food you must use the airport facilities.

Nearly every train, other than London–Brighton fast trains, calls at Gatwick. The main service is the air-conditioned 'Gatwick Express' non-stop to London Victoria, taking thirty minutes and running every fifteen minutes during the day. But there are also hourly through trains to most stations from Hastings to Portsmouth, and also to Reading via Redhill, Dorking, and Guildford. There are also a few long-distance InterCity trains to Birmingham, Manchester, and Liverpool via Kensington Olympia. From May 1988 the new 'Thameslink' will provide a service (via a reopened tunnel in the City of London) to King's Cross and on to St Albans, Luton, and Bedford.

One is, however, now about to enter Sussex where the real interest of the line begins. The line continues as four tracks as far as the entrance to Balcombe Tunnel. But in view of the extensive tunnelling and civil engineering features necessary to get the line to the coast, the company never found the wherewithal to enlarge its capacity beyond this point.

On leaving Gatwick the full size and grandeur of the airport becomes apparent on the right-hand side, dominated by carriage sidings, warehouses, a massive radar scanner, and with very little countryside as we approach the post-war satellite town of Crawley.

The town itself is served by **Three Bridges**, a bustling railway junction when Crawley was only a small village. It is now the nerve centre of the railway system in this area with the new signalling centre which controls 280 track miles from Anerley and Thornton Heath to the South Coast. Although it has five platforms, the station architecture is uninspiring. To the south are more sidings on both sides of the track and while the line to Horsham and Littlehampton (described in Chapter 8) can clearly be observed diverging on the right, traces of the former line to East Grinstead and Tunbridge Wells can barely be discerned among the tracks on the left.

After a fairly flat stretch from Redhill, the line now reaches the next major obstacle the LBSCR had to surmount on its route to the coast – The Weald – and as the line enters Tilgate Forest it is mainly in cutting until Balcombe Tunnel (1141 yards).

**Balcombe** Station is not very prepossessing, but does have some pleasing buildings on the up platform. The village it serves has no special attractions for the visitor, despite possessing the most rural setting of any place served by the Brighton mainline. But it is the best stopping-off point for a walk into the Ouse Valley and a view of the viaduct there; minor roads can be followed all the way to Haywards Heath.

The most dramatic part of the line follows as the train races across the 100-foot-high thirty-seven-arch Ouse Valley Viaduct, built of stone and flanked with imposing pavilions at either end. There are good rural views on each side. Just before the line plunges into a cutting note the former line from Horsted Keynes coming in from the left at Copyhold Junction. For a short time visitors could take a train from Haywards Heath to the preserved Bluebell Railway, until the branch line fell to the Beeching Axe in 1963; but there is still a bus service in lieu from this point (for details see Chapter 2).

**Haywards Heath** is quite a pleasing four-platform station serving this sizeable Sussex town, with its cattle market clearly visible to the right. The station canopies and entrance hall are typical of Southern Railway design. There is a buffet on the down (Brighton) island platform. The station also has a large car park, reflecting its importance as a commuter station. Through the short Folly Tunnel one now emerges from The Weald into flat rolling countryside. As the train leaves the cutting, a brief glimpse of the South Downs appears on the right before the train enters **Wivelsfield** – a bare concrete structure with basic shelter.

Shortly afterwards the line to Lewes (described in Chapter 5) diverges to the left at Keymer Junction and we arrive at **Burgess Hill** – the main station serving this centre of population. This is a somewhat more pleasing mid-Victorian structure with attractive canopies and it is from here that the most dramatic views of the South Downs appear on both sides of the track.

**Hassocks** is another basic concrete station, but its importance lies in its position at the foot of the Downs. It makes an ideal starting-point for rambles or cycle rides on the Downs, with Ditchling Beacon, Walstonbury Hill, the two Clayton windmills 'Jack and Jill', and the Devil's Dyke easily accessible. The nearest of all are Jack and Jill, reached by a footpath to Clayton along the left-hand side of the railway and then a bridle-path up the scarp slope from the other end of the village of Clayton; there is a good viewpoint by the windmills (see also Chapter 5 for a fuller description of this part of the South Downs). Hassocks and the other intermediate stations between Haywards Heath and Brighton now enjoy two semi-fast trains per hour to London – one to Victoria and one to London Bridge.

Now we make the final ascent to Clayton Tunnel (at 2259 yards, the longest on this line). Note particularly the impressive crenellated portal standing like a fort as the gateway to Brighton, not matched by one at the other end.

As the line continues through rolling downland, mainly in a cutting, observe to the right for a moment the windmill at Westdene, before the train plunges into the short Patcham Tunnel and finally emerges at **Preston Park** on the outskirts of Brighton.

The rest of the journey is typical of the approach to most major railway termini. The line to Hove and Worthing veers off sharply to the right into a tunnel and beyond are the former Pullman workshops, now occupied by preserved railway stock including that owned by the Southern Electric Group.

Just before entering **Brighton**'s extensive nine-platform station (built in 1840 by David Mocatta), the line from Lewes sweeps in surreptitiously from the left on an impressive twenty-seven-arch viaduct barely discernible among the maze of sidings. The curving platforms are surmounted by a magnificent two-bay train shed, worthy of comparison with York and Bristol Temple Meads, and now in the early stages of a sorely needed refurbishment. Brighton is the only traditional seaside town on the South Coast to have an overall roof.

The Space Age bookstall and impressive tubular-framed departure board are a bit of a cultural shock to the architectural purist, but together with the information kiosk and bureau de change below it are an undoubted boon to the travellers who throng its portals. There is also a spacious fast-food buffet (though nothing for the more discerning eater) and a modern travel centre.

# BRIGHTON
### By H. Trevor Jones

The railway made Brighton very much what it is today, making possible cheap fast travel for Londoners to the seaside. The building of hotels like the Grand (recently much rebuilt after a terrorist bomb attack during the Conservative Party Conference of 1984) and the Metropole reflect this.

On leaving the station to reach the sea-front, you keep straight on for ¾ mile down Queens Road, which becomes West Street; or you can take a frequent little shuttle bus two-thirds of the way, ending up at the Churchill Square shopping centre, the terminus of a large number of bus routes on weekdays. There are also several bus routes from the station to the Palace Pier, which can be reached on foot by turning left at the sea-front. This substantial structure is the larger of Brighton's two piers and the only one currently fully open to the public, although a section of the smaller West Pier has now been reopened. At the end of the Palace Pier is a good view inland as well as fine coastal views on a clear day, and there are many of the usual attractions along its length. There is even a museum where you can buy and use old pre-decimalisation penny (1d) coins in appropriate historical slot-machines.

The beach at Brighton is completely shingle – except at low spring tide when a narrow strip of sand appears, and that usually only in the early morning or late afternoon or evening! Sea-bathing commenced in Brighton in 1750 on the advice of a Dr Russell, who extolled its medicinal properties.

There are plenty of attractions inviting you to spend money all along the front, below the main promenade road. Eastwards from the Palace Pier is the Volks Electric Railway, which is the oldest electric railway in the world and is now owned by Brighton Corporation. It provides a frequent summer service to a point just short of the Brighton Marina which was recently constructed to cater for the many privately owned boats in the area and lies about a mile along the sea-front. Volks also built a railway on an underwater track powered by an overhead cable which opened in 1896, but closed four years later because of frequent breakdowns.

Just inland from the Palace Pier is Old Steine, which is a sort of square with a little parkland in the middle and round which are the terminal points of many bus routes as well as a bus travel office. At its inland end, on the left (west) side, is the famous and architecturally exotic Royal Pavilion, commissioned by George IV when Prince Regent and largely the work of John Nash. The Pavilion, begun in 1784 and completed in 1822, has an Oriental exterior and a still more amazing Chinese interior, and is open daily to the public.

The other major non-maritime attraction at Brighton is the charming Old Town, known as 'The Lanes', between the sea-front and the Pavilion. These are a criss-cross of narrow red-brick-paved alleyways, safe from the noise of traffic, in which are clustered a fascinating collection of antique shops, pubs, and cafés. This spot formed the heart of the original medieval fishing village, known as Brighthelmstone.

Also worth a visit is the Brighton Aquarium situated on the front (Madeira Drive) between the Palace Pier and the Volks Electric Railway terminus. Near by is the finishing-point of the famous London to Brighton 'Old Crocks' (Veteran Car) Rally, which usually takes place on the first Sunday in November.

Inland from Brighton is the Devil's Dyke which is a viewpoint nearly 700 feet high on top of the South Downs escarpment. In summer it can be reached by an open-top bus that runs along the coast from Rottingdean (east of the Marina), through Brighton, and on to Hove, before turning inland to go on to the Downs. There is a large café and a souvenir shop at Devil's Dyke, as well as plenty of walking opportunities, not least along the South Downs Way itself.

# 2

# EAST CROYDON–EAST GRINSTEAD
## by Laurence Skinnerton and Graham Collett

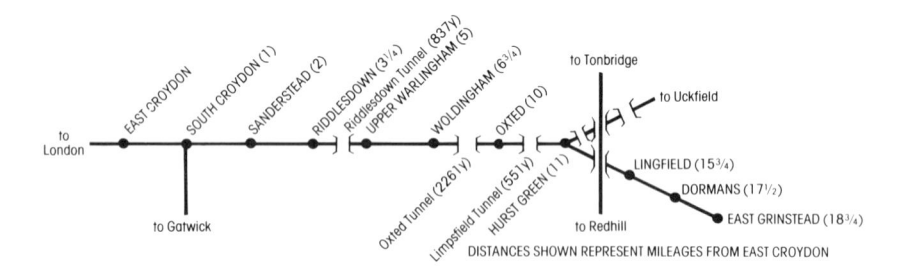

The line from South Croydon Junction (on the main London–Brighton line) to East Grinstead was opened on 10 March 1884, being partly owned by the LBSCR and partly by the SER. After earlier fears that the line would not be electrified until its diesel stock had become life expired, approval was given for electrification and re-signalling between Sanderstead and East Grinstead. Following a special 'Gala Week-end' to publicise the new electric service, the £8,000,000 project was formally inaugurated by the Secretary of State for Transport on 30 September 1987, and the new service commenced on Monday, 5 October. Notable improvements included faster journey times and a more frequent off-peak service.

Croydon, originally a separate town, was enveloped by the Greater London conurbation in the late 1930s. It now has a population of about 300,000 and is twinned with Arnhem in Holland. The Croydon Canal, which had twenty-eight locks between

Croydon and the Thames, terminated in a basin on the site of the present West Croydon Station. The canal was replaced by an atmospheric railway which ran until the early 1840s, when it was itself replaced by a conventional railway with steam locomotives.

Croydon is now a major business and commercial centre with two leading theatres – the Fairfield Hall and the Ashcroft. There is also a smaller theatre – the Warehouse – specialising in 'fringe theatre', which is very close to East Croydon Station. The town has been comprehensively redeveloped with office blocks, underpasses, dual carriageways, and a major shopping complex – the Whitgift Centre.

Leaving **East Croydon** (usually from Platforms 5 or 6) the train passes through a high brick-lined cutting on its journey to East Grinstead. After 1 mile the cutting opens out and the line enters **South Croydon** Station. To the left can be seen the bridge carrying the former line from Woodside (on the Mid-Kent line) to Selsdon and Sanderstead, closed to passenger trains in 1983. However, the line is still used by weekly oil trains to the depot at Selsdon and may be included in a light rail system proposed for the Croydon area.

The train leaves the main Brighton line (described in Chapter 1) at **South Croydon**, and then follows a south-easterly direction. It continues on to the site of **Selsdon** Station, where the East Grinstead platforms closed in 1917, and the remainder in 1983 with the withdrawal of the Woodside–Sanderstead service.

The line passes allotments on the right and some 1930s mock-Tudor dwellings, prior to reaching **Sanderstead** Station (1 mile from South Croydon) on a ruling gradient of 1 in 83. This station has recently been rebuilt as part of the electrification and modernisation scheme for the line.

The gradient then changes to 1 in 100 up to **Riddlesdown**, 1¼ miles farther on. At Riddlesdown the line climbs on to an embankment, passing over a residential road. This leads on the left to a shopping parade and on the right to a residential development.

The train enters Riddlesdown Tunnel, 837 yards long, and then climbs again until, after ½ mile, it reaches Riddlesdown Viaduct. The viaduct consists of five spans of wrought-iron girders lying on brick piers. The line continues to climb on a ledge on the side of Caterham Valley, which is U-shaped. From the right of the train the Caterham line can be seen on the valley floor, as can the A22 Eastbourne road.

After passing Riddlesdown golf-course on the left, the line rises on an embankment to cross the Whyteleafe to Warlingham road and then enters **Upper Warlingham** Station. This station (which is ¼ mile diagonally opposite Whyteleafe Station on the Caterham line) and the next station, Woldingham, are of SER design.

On leaving Upper Warlingham, the line curves away along the side of a hill. It continues to climb through the North Downs, eventually tunnelling through them between Woldingham and Oxted. The environment gradually changes from an urban to a rural one. The train passes under a road and the countryside opens out, leaving behind the settlements along the valley. The line crosses Woldingham Viaduct, which carries it over a minor road leading to the village of Woldingham, and soon enters **Woldingham** Station.

The station is surrounded by trees and undulating countryside and makes an ideal starting-point for rambles. A particularly attractive walk is to follow the bridleway past Marden Park Farm and Winders Hill to join the North Downs Way (some steep climbing is involved) and thence over the M25 (a special footbridge has been provided) and down into Godstone village. An alternative, less strenuous, route back to the railway at either Oxted or Hurst Green stations is afforded by taking the footpath to Godstone Church and thence via Leigh Place, Tandridge, and Broadham Green.

The line continues for another 2 miles, gradually running into a deep cutting and

Oxted Station, seen on the Gala Week-end held to launch the new electric service (Photo: Graham Collett)

then entering Oxted Tunnel, which is 2,261 yards long. On leaving the tunnel the line passes under the M25 and, after passing the former Oxted lime-works on the left and the parish church on the right, enters **Oxted** Station.

Oxted lies on the A25 Godstone–Westerham road which, although relatively quiet now, was extremely busy on summer week-ends prior to the opening of the M25. The station is in the middle of New Oxted, which is separate from Old Oxted, lying ½ mile to the west. New Oxted is mainly of Late Victorian/Edwardian origin, but the principal building style is of the 1930s. The town centre is built in a style similar to that of Old Oxted, which dates from the sixteenth century (although the parish church dates from AD 986).

Oxted Station has recently been rebuilt in Swiss Chalet style. Immediately south of the station, the line runs over the viaduct which divides Oxted from Limpsfield and descends into Limpsfield Tunnel. About ¼ mile south of the tunnel lies **Hurst Green** Station. This station was built in 1961 to replace the original halt (south of the road bridge), which was constructed in 1907 to serve the then hamlet of Hurst Green. Although Hurst Green is now more akin to a suburb of Oxted, it retains the air of a rural village, with open country to the west and footpaths leading off in all directions.

The Uckfield line diverges just south of the station, at Hurst Green Junction (see Chapter 3 for further details of this line). Meanwhile the East Grinstead line passes out into gentle countryside and gradually enters the flood plain of the River Eden. However, before the Eden is reached, the train passes the hamlet of Merle Common to the east. It continues in a straight line, descending all the time to allow the Redhill–Tonbridge line (described in Chapter 4) to cross over the East Grinstead route. Shortly before the Redhill–Tonbridge line is reached, there used to be a connecting line, known as the 'Crowhurst Spur'.

The train continues south; after passing under an overbridge, on the western side is the former Crowhurst brickworks – now closed and used for a landfill site. The line continues, following a gentle curve through open countryside before reaching **Lingfield** Station.

The village of Lingfield has a population of 8,000 and the station is at the eastern end of the town. It is on the edge of the River Eden flood plain and is sometimes subject to flooding. The station is built in the LBSCR style and dates from 1884, as do the SER stations referred to earlier. Lingfield Racecourse, which was constructed in 1890, is located ¼ mile to the west of the station. On race days the station is very busy, with between 500 and 1,000 passengers leaving and joining trains (which usually include one or two extras for racegoers); the station originally had an extra platform for races traffic.

From Lingfield, the line climbs continuously, being carried on an embankment. Crossing Racecourse Road, the line leaves the Eden flood plain and passes to the west of the village of Dormansland. After passing under a bridge, **Dormans** Station is reached. It is situated in a shallow cutting, with the station building at road-level next to the road bridge over the railway. This station, which was reopened experimentally on Sundays with the introduction of the new electric service, provides a good starting-point for walks in this very pleasant area.

On leaving Dormans, the train passes through a cutting and under a bridge linking the two halves of the Dormans Park private estate. The cutting opens out and the train crosses an embankment before it reaches Cook's Mill Pond Viaduct, which carries the line over an artificial lake. The line continues on to the outskirts of East Grinstead, where it curves past housing estates and passes under a road bridge at the former St Margaret's Junction. This is the point where the former East Grinstead High Level line, closed in 1967, diverged from the existing route. After passing under two bridges, the present line enters **East Grinstead** Station.

The present station is a single-storey structure, erected in 1972 to replace the 1883 buildings, which had high-level and low-level platforms. Trains from London were able to serve both levels until closure of the line from St Margaret's Junction (referred to above). The remains of the abutments of the High Level Station can still be seen at the north end of the present platforms. The High Level platforms were built to serve the Three Bridges–Tunbridge Wells line, another casualty of the Beeching era which has since been converted into a public footpath and bridleway. The section from East Grinstead to Three Bridges is known as the Worth Way, while the trackbed extending eastwards as far as Groombridge, where it meets the Wealden line (see Chapter 3), has become the Forest Way Country Park.

East Grinstead is a pleasant market town with a population of 25,000, and a well-known Burns Unit of Second World War origin (situated at the Queen Victoria Hospital). It has a High Street dating from 1340 and is a centre for the surrounding area, with buses to Brighton, Crawley, and Tunbridge Wells. Some buses, such as Nos. 239/639 and 291/691 (two different routes to Tunbridge Wells – see also Chapter 3) serve the railway station and town centre. Other routes only serve the town centre – some ten to fifteen minutes away on foot (turn right out of the station forecourt, then half-right into Railway Approach and right into London Road).

# THE BLUEBELL RAILWAY
### By Laurence Skinnerton and Graham Collett

Originally part of the line which connected East Grinstead to Lewes, the county town of East Sussex (described in Chapter 5), the railway was opened in 1882 and closed by BR in 1958. In the following year the Bluebell Railway Preservation Society was formed and ran its first train on 7 August 1960, with an engine at each end and two elderly coaches sandwiched between them. Since then, over 5,000,000 people have taken a steam-hauled ride between **Horsted Keynes** (originally from a temporary halt just south of the present station) and **Sheffield Park**, a distance of 5 miles. The Bluebell now has some thirty historic locomotives (including six which are over a hundred years old) and a comprehensive collection of coaches and wagons.

Trains run daily during the summer months, at week-ends during the spring and autumn, and on Sundays throughout the year. On peak Sundays and Bank Holidays the service is approximately one train every thirty minutes. For details of train services telephone Newick (082 572) 2370 or for other enquiries ring Newick 3777.

Sheffield Park Station is authentically restored in the Late Victorian style of the LBSCR, while Horsted Keynes presents an imposing glimpse of Southern Railway 1930s elegance. Sheffield Park has a new purpose-designed catering building to match the 1880s station. This serves a large variety of refreshments from a cup of tea to a full meal. Horsted Keynes has a Victorian refreshment room serving snacks and light refreshments. Full bar facilities are provided at both stations.

The Bluebell Railway has now obtained planning permission for its proposed extension of the line northwards to East Grinstead. The proposed terminus is adjacent to Platform 1 at East Grinstead Station. It has purchased the site of the former station at West Hoathly and more recently the station at Kingscote. Some of the former trackbed is in private ownership and the public are asked not to trespass.

Kingscote Station, which is situated some 2 miles south of East Grinstead on Vowels Lane, is currently being restored to 1950s condition by volunteers. The station can be reached by London Country buses Nos 434 and 473 every half hour from East Grinstead Station on weekdays only – alight at Station Road, Kingscote and continue ahead where the main road turns right; or you can walk from East Grinstead by simply following the Turners Hill road (B2110). Special buses from East Grinstead to Horsted Keynes (see below) sometimes call at Kingscote Station.

It is possible to reach the Bluebell by bus from East Grinstead Station (No. 270 – not on Sundays). This service runs every two hours to Horsted Keynes and then continues on to Haywards Heath. This bus does not serve the station, so it is necessary to walk approximately 1 mile from Horsted Keynes village (the route is clearly signposted). However, a special bus, the Emsworth and District No. 36, usually operates from East Grinstead Station to Horsted Keynes Station, on certain summer Sundays. In 1987 it operated at approximately monthly intervals and provided reasonable connections with BR trains at East Grinstead. For timetable information telephone Emsworth and District (Emsworth 376886). Buses also usually run on 'Special Events Days' at the Bluebell and sometimes serve Kingscote and West Hoathly stations (see above) *en route*. Please ring Newick 3777 for details.

An easier way of reaching the Bluebell by rail is by special bus (Southdown No. 769) from Haywards Heath to Sheffield Park Station. This is the route usually advised by BR. The service operates on summer Sundays and Bank Holidays and daily during August (further details are given in the BR timetable). Return bus tickets, inclusive of a return trip on the Bluebell and offering an attractive discount, are available from the BR Travel Centre at Haywards Heath. A regular bus service (No. 270) – referred to above – also operates on weekdays.

# 3

## THE WEALDEN LINE: OXTED–EDENBRIDGE–UCKFIELD

### By John Bigny and A. Raleigh Mordaunt

The section of line between Oxted and Uckfield is commonly known as the 'Uckfield line'. This and the Dorking to Horsham route are the only complete sections of line described in this book that do not (at the time of writing) have a Sunday train service.

To reach **Oxted** (in Surrey) one would most likely travel from London Victoria, although there is also a regular service from London Bridge. In either case the route

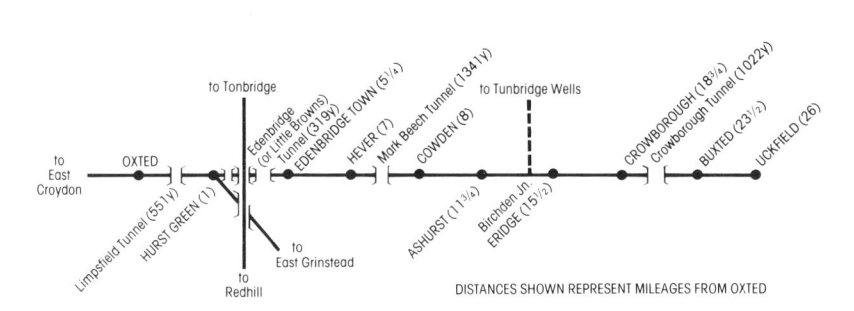

```
                                                                    to Tunbridge Wells
              to Tonbridge                                                                    CROWBOROUGH (18¼)
                      Edenbridge                    HEVER (7)   Mark Beech Tunnel (13¼)                Crowborough Tunnel (10 22)
                      (or Little Browns)                                                                            BUXTED (23½)    UCKFIELD (26)
                      Tunnel (3 19)    EDENBRIDGE TOWN (5¼)     COWDEN (8)
  to          OXTED
  East
  Croydon                                                                          Birchden Jn.
                         Limpsfield Tunnel (55 v)   HURST GREEN (1)    ASHURST (11¾)   ERIDGE (15½)
                                                   to
                                                   East Grinstead
                                         to
                                         Redhill                  DISTANCES SHOWN REPRESENT MILEAGES FROM OXTED
```

(described in more detail in Chapter 2) is via East Croydon, where interchange can be made with most mainline services between London and the Sussex coast. Except for a few peak trains, you will in any case have to change from an electric train to a diesel at Oxted. Uckfield trains normally start from the bay platform (No. 3) at Oxted.

The journey time from Oxted to Uckfield is approximately fifty-five minutes. The stations of Oxted and Hurst Green are in Surrey; Edenbridge Town, Hever, Cowden, and Ashurst are in Kent; and Eridge, Crowborough, Buxted, and Uckfield are in East Sussex. This divided interest in the line has not helped its development, although BR does its best, running an hourly off-peak service. However, work on a £2,500,000 modernisation scheme, involving the installation of modern signalling and the singling of some sections of track, is due to commence later this year. BR also plan to publish (summer 1988) a series of leaflets, prepared by Mr Mordaunt, describing walks from stations on the line.

On leaving Oxted (20½ miles from Victoria) the train crosses a viaduct over the A25, and then passes through a short tunnel to reach **Hurst Green.** Between Hurst Green and **Edenbridge Town** Station you travel through rich agricultural land and enter the county of Kent before entering a tunnel as the town of Edenbridge is approached. In this tunnel there is a short gap where the Redhill–Tonbridge line crosses above it. Edenbridge Town Station (not to be confused with plain Edenbridge Station, known locally as the 'Top' station, on the other line – see Chapter 4) is conveniently situated, in that on leaving the station you walk along Station Approach and turn left into the High Street, which has shops of varying architecture. At the southern end of the High Street there is a road bridge which crosses the River Eden. There are a number of light industrial firms in Edenbridge producing such items as glass bottles, coat-hangers, and BR station signs. The population has grown considerably in recent years due to public and private sector housing schemes.

One major attraction is the Edenbridge Bonfire Society Parade of Floats and Firework Display, which is usually held on the Saturday evening nearest to 5 November. The Parade commences at Spitals Cross estate, Four Elms Road, off the east side of the main road in between the two railways. The Parade ends at the Recreation Ground in Lingfield Road, where a huge bonfire with an effigy of Guy Fawkes is lit, and there is a colourful firework display.

**Buses:** From Edenbridge, serving both its stations, there is a roughly hourly bus (Maidstone & District Nos 231 and 233) giving a half-hour ride to the pretty little village of Penshurst (see Chapter 4). The buses continue by two different routes to Tunbridge Wells, taking another half an hour, so that the full journey is better done by train from the 'Top' station, changing at Tonbridge. South of Penshurst the No. 231 bus takes a particularly pretty route along the upper reaches of the River Medway, signposted for motorists as the 'High Weald Tour' and then approaches Tunbridge Wells (see *KESR*) via Langton Green and past Rusthall and Tunbridge Wells commons.

South of Edenbridge, the line runs though exceptionally beautiful scenery all the way to Uckfield. The area is also interesting geologically. After Wealden Clay down to Edenbridge the Hastings Beds are crossed giving a variety of hard sandstones – the Tun Wells producing the rocks around Eridge and the Ashdown either side of Crowborough – together with pockets of sand, Wadhurst Clay, and alluvial soils all adding variety to the landscape. The line descends on steep gradients to the River Eden at Edenbridge, climbs on equally steep gradients through Hever to Markbeech Tunnel, and then descends more gently past Cowden to the Upper Medway Valley at Ashurst. Then follows a fairly level stretch to Eridge, after which there is a steep climb round the side of Ashdown Forest to Crowborough Tunnel and finally a steep drop down to Buxted and Uckfield.

On leaving Edenbridge the River Eden, a tributary of the Medway, is crossed, and then the line climbs dead straight on an embankment, affording good views to the left on a clear day of the Greensand Ridge escarpment, with its three peaks, from left to right, of Crockham Hill, Toy's Hill, and Ide Hill, all of which are National Trust properties. The next station is **Hever**, with its famous castle dating back to about 1270. It was in fact Hever Castle where Henry VIII came to woo Anne Boleyn. In the early part of this century it was occupied by the Astor family. In addition to the castle there is a magnificent 30-acre garden. The castle and gardens are usually open from April to the end of September, except on Thursdays. For further details concerning the castle and gardens, together with particulars about other events held there, telephone Edenbridge (0732) 865224.

To reach Hever Castle, leave Hever Station by the down (ticket-office) side. You are then in Station Approach. A few yards down on your right is Sandfield Cottage and at its gate is a map of the route. It is a fifteen- to twenty-minute walk to the castle gate. Turning right as you leave Station Approach is the slightly shorter route. Turning left as you leave Station Approach takes you past some rather more attractive and interesting houses.

Beyond Hever the line passes through Mark Beech Woods and then Mark Beech Tunnel, 1,341 yards long, and comes out in the High Weald at **Cowden**. The station is about ½ mile from the village of Cowden. There are no main roads here, only country lanes. Taking the lane uphill gives some pleasant views over the valley and leads to the inn at Markbeech or onwards by delightful cross-country paths to Chiddingstone with its castle, Castle Inn, and medieval village owned by the National Trust, at a distance of about 3 miles from Cowden Station. From Hever to Eridge the surrounding area is excellent for walking, with numerous footpaths and bridleways marked on the local Ordnance Survey map. Some good walks can be devised by starting at one station and ending at another.

The train, however, descends to the Upper Medway Valley, crossing the river just before **Ashurst** Station, now an unstaffed halt. Although there are no trains on Sundays, you can actually get here seven days a week by the No. 239/639 bus. This provides a two-hourly service from Tunbridge Wells to East Grinstead (replacing this section of the former No. 900 bus from Chatham to Gatwick Airport referred to in *KESR*) and passes through pleasant hilly countryside between Ashurst and East Grinstead.

To the right of the train are views towards the lovely villages of Withyham and Hartfield, with, on the horizon, Gill's Lap Clump, a viewpoint on the north side of Ashdown Forest. The railway follows the River Medway for a mile or so south of Ashurst, until the site of Ashurst Junction is reached where, until 1967, there used to be a line from East Grinstead coming in behind you on the right and going off ahead on the left to Tunbridge Wells. The trackbed from Groombridge to East Grinstead (see Chapter 2) has now been converted into a footpath and bridleway – the Forest Way Country Park.

A Victoria-Uckfield train arrives at Eridge, formerly the junction for the Tunbridge Wells line (currently the subject of a reopening campaign) (Photo: Tom Heavyside)

A little farther on is the site of Birchden Junction where the Tunbridge Wells–Eridge line used to come in behind you on the left until it was closed on 6 July 1985 after a strong local fight, which even went to the courts. The Tunbridge Wells and Eridge Railway Preservation Society was formed in August 1985 by some of those who objected to the line's closure and wanted to see the public service reinstated. The Society will, *inter alia*, be allowed one of the two tracks from Birchden to Eridge and envisages operating a public service through to Tunbridge Wells on weekdays, supplemented at week-ends by vintage steam and diesel trains. The closed line served **Groombridge**, a pleasant village divided by the Kent and Sussex border, where the Preservation Society has recently opened an exhibition centre, railway shop, and buffet in the old station building. For further details of the Society, write to: The Membership Secretary, 57 Farm Fields, Sanderstead, Surrey CR2 0HR.

Farther along the closed line is High Rocks, an interesting venue for visitors, with its scenic rock walks. The Society plans to revive High Rocks Halt, closed in 1952. The preserved railway will terminate at the old engine shed on the **Tunbridge Wells West** Station site, by courtesy of Sainsburys who are developing most of the redundant railway land there. The old station building which is listed, will become a restaurant. Sufficient unbuilt-on space will remain to protect the railway right-of-way onwards to BR **Tunbridge Wells Central**, distant some ½ mile, just in case future generations can persuade BR to reconnect with the West Station. The preservation scheme has received much support from local MPs and councillors and local authority financial involvement is being sought.

Approaching **Eridge**, along this pleasant tributary of the River Medway, there is marvellous scenery on the left. Harrison's Rocks, often used by trainee mountain-climbers, can be seen in the background, along with Birchden Wood. Ramblers can reach the rocks by walking back from Eridge Station along a lane on the south-west side of the railway and using a farm crossing at Forge Farm to get across the line, although the entrance for climbers is on a minor road south from Groombridge.

**Eridge** Station, peacefully situated in the middle of green fields 1 mile from Birchden Junction, used to be an important junction; but today the only connections are the Maidstone & District Nos. 228 and 229 buses and the joint Maidstone & District/Southdown No. 729 bus from Tunbridge Wells to Brighton, giving two buses an hour along the A26 between Crowborough Cross (the central crossroads) and Tunbridge Wells. From Eridge Station, the beauty-spots of the Warren and Eridge Park can be reached by turning left outside the station and walking or taking a bus for a mile uphill to the village of Eridge Green. There is a pleasant walk right through Eridge Park, past some attractive lakes, to the village of Frant, from where another bus can be taken or a further pleasant walk on the footpath to Tunbridge Wells (see *KESR*).

For those who want to walk a section of the Wealdway long-distance footpath from Gravesend to Eastbourne, Eridge makes an excellent starting-point. Follow various footpaths and minor roads westwards to pick up the Wealdway at Fisher's Gate, about 1½ miles south of Withyham and just north of Five Hundred Acre Wood – well known to readers of A. A. Milne who lived near by. The path crosses the ridges of Ashdown Forest with magnificent views, and you can return from Buxted or Uckfield Station.

South of Eridge Station, the junction of the former Cuckoo line to Eastbourne is still discernible. Our line follows the same Medway tributary, now a fine rocky stream, as far as **Crowborough and Jarvis Brook** Station, which is actually situated at Jarvis Brook rather than Crowborough. Although Crowborough has a local bus from this station, the centre is better served by bus from Eridge. Crowborough is a residential town with a growing population. Indeed it is one of the largest inland towns in East Sussex and has one of the biggest comprehensive schools in the country – The Beacon – with some 2,000 pupils.

South of Crowborough is another quite long tunnel, which is one of the highest points reached by rail in south-east England, after which the line descends steeply through beautiful Wealden country. But however peacefully rural the scenery now appears, it is of interest to remember that, prior to the advent of the Industrial Revolution in northern England, The Weald itself was a prime industrial region using charcoal from the surrounding forests together with water-power from the many streams, for smelting iron.

The site of these old ironworks can be seen just below Sleeches Viaduct on the left, about 2 miles beyond the tunnel. Some 2 miles up the valley to the left can be found Huggett's Furnace, the site of the works and hammer-pond of Ralph Hogge at Buxted, who is said to have cast the first cannon in this country; his house can be seen near Buxted Church. Many of the cannon used to maintain Britain's naval supremacy came from this region, as did the railings round St Paul's Cathedral in London, which actually came from Ashburnham 4 miles west of Battle.

It is an interesting turn of events that also from Sleeches Viaduct could be seen for a while the derrick of an exploratory oil-well being drilled on the famous Sleeches geological fault, about ½ mile to the left. There is another fine viaduct, Greenhurst, crossing the headwaters of the River Uck, about a mile farther on. Both viaducts are named after local farms.

Next comes **Buxted**. The village on the left side of the railway is of no special interest, but if you turn right into the A272 and go under the railway bridge, you will soon come to a side entrance to Buxted Park on the left, through which run several pleasant public footpaths. One path follows near a small stream parallel to the railway, making a direct walk to Uckfield, while another, at only an angle from the main road, takes you to the attractive old Buxted Parish Church of St Margaret the Queen. The church is next to the main country house in the middle of the park, which was no doubt fine for the lord of the manor or local squire, but less convenient for the ordinary villagers until the advent of the motor car. Approaching the park is an avenue of 200-year-old Scots pines, and a famous herd of fallow deer roam freely around.

The journey by train is completed with a short run alongside the River Uck (a tributary of the Ouse that goes out to sea at Newhaven) to a level crossing over the busy A22 into the **Uckfield** terminus, 46 miles from London Victoria. This does not look like a terminus because, of course, it was not one until the line onwards to Lewes was closed. There has been talk for a number of years of building a new station on the opposite side of the A22, to allow removal of the level crossing. In any case there is already a new bypass round the town. Like Oxted, Uckfield also has a cinema, which is situated on the High Street going up a hill. Uckfield is an excellent shopping centre, arguably the best between Tunbridge Wells and Brighton.

**Buses:** The aforementioned hourly No. 729 bus now supplemented by other local buses, takes twenty minutes from Uckfield to Lewes bus station, which is ten minutes' walk from Lewes railway station and through to Brighton the bus takes almost one hour. The other way it is forty-two minutes to Tunbridge Wells. This bus even runs on Sundays, although only every two hours. Other local buses leaving from Uckfield are No. 781, two-hourly to Haywards Heath on the London–Brighton mainline, taking three-quarters of an hour; occasional buses to East Grinstead, taking about forty minutes; the No. 781 (the other way) to Hailsham (twenty-five to thirty minutes) and Eastbourne (forty-five to fifty-five minutes) and the No. 728 to Eastbourne via Heathfield (twenty-two minutes) and Hailsham (fifty-two minutes). This last service provides good views as the bus travels along several ridge-top roads to Heathfield.

## The Lavender Line

South of Uckfield, mention must be made of the Isfield Steam Railway Company's **Lavender Line** based on the one-time BR station at Isfield on the former rail route from Uckfield to Lewes. Isfield Station and an adjoining section of line were purchased privately by the Milham family in the summer of 1983. In less than eighteen months they had completely restored the station, signal-box, and adjoining buildings to form a fully operative museum, complete with engines and carriages. Steam-hauled rides are given every Sunday from March to December and on Bank Holiday Mondays. For further information contact the Isfield Steam Railway Company, Station House, Isfield Station, near Uckfield, East Sussex TN22 5XB (telephone Isfield 515).

Isfield is currently served by alternate No. 729 buses on their way to Lewes and Brighton. There is a strong body of local opinion that would like BR to restore the Uckfield–Lewes rail link; indeed BR itself is quite interested provided the local authorities, or anyone else, contribute £4,500,000 towards a total cost of £6,000,000

The Lavender Line operates on a section of the former Uckfield–Lewes rail route (Photo: Tom Heavyside)

— a mere pittance compared with what is spent or might be spent on road improvements. It is understood that a BR single-track line could co-exist harmoniously with railway preservation activities on the Lavender line, given goodwill all round.

# 4
# TONBRIDGE–REDHILL
## by Mark Bigny

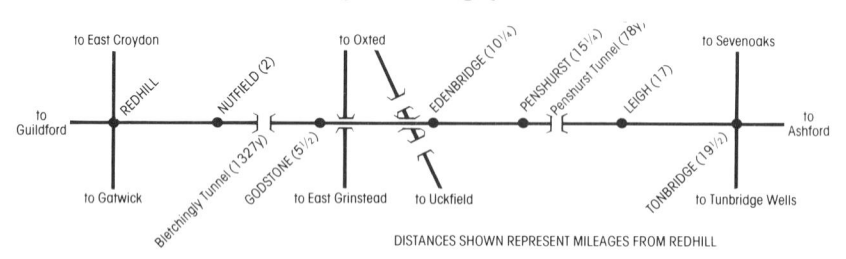

DISTANCES SHOWN REPRESENT MILEAGES FROM REDHILL

This line forms part of the cross-country railway line which stretches from Tonbridge to Reading, via Redhill, Dorking, and Guildford, providing on its way a number of useful links. It is one of the oldest lines in south-east England, being opened in 1842. In the early 1920s the line served a unique purpose; pilots flying from London to Paris followed the railway tracks to the coast, as at that time aircraft had no proper navigational aids. To assist the pilots, Redhill and Tonbridge stations had their names painted in large letters on their roofs.

During the Second World War, the line saw 'its finest hour' in 1940; at the time of the evacuation from Dunkirk, 565 special trains used the route from 27 May to 4 June. The line is likely to become important again in the future, as Channel Tunnel traffic puts pressure on the direct routes from Kent into London. Indeed, it is proposed to electrify the Tonbridge–Redhill section for Channel Tunnel freight traffic, which will reach the Midlands and the North via the Brighton mainline and Kensington Olympia.

The present service from Tonbridge to Reading is run for most of the day in two overlapping sections: Tonbridge–Redhill–Reigate and Gatwick Airport–Redhill–Reading. Trains are timed to connect with each other at Redhill, but there are also some through trains from Tonbridge to Reading. All intermediate stations on this part of the line are unmanned, passengers obtaining their tickets from the conductor guard.

The train will probably be formed of a three-car 'Cross-Country'-type DMU, which with their large windows give passengers good views of the scenery. The train will usually be standing in Platform 1A at **Tonbridge**, which is the platform farthest from the footbridge. Tonbridge Station is also served by the Charing Cross–Ashford–Dover service and the Charing Cross–Tunbridge Wells–Hastings service (both described in *KESR*) and during the day many people change trains here.

Tonbridge itself is quite old and is situated on the River Medway. The town has grown considerably in this century, but retains many old buildings and the remains of its castle. The station is situated close to the main shopping area and only a short walk from the castle. Turn left out of the booking-office, walk up through the High

Street and the castle remains are on the left after crossing the River Medway. Near the castle, part of which now houses the District Council offices, is a group of fifteenth-century buildings. There are pleasant walks beside the river and round the castle grounds and adjacent parkland. At the north end of the High Street, housed in an imposing building, is the famous Tonbridge School, founded in 1553 by Sir Andrew Judd. At the other end of the town is the Judd School, founded by the Skinners' Company in 1888, and now serving as the local boys' grammar school.

On leaving **Tonbridge**, the train takes the line on the far left past Tonbridge West goods yard. It is immediately noticeable how straight the line is and in fact there are only two or three curves all the way to Redhill. Shortly after passing the goods yard, you will get your first view of the River Medway and its tributaries, and during the fishing season this is a popular place for anglers. Because of the river the area is very susceptible to flooding and a number of flood-prevention measures have been taken; these can be clearly seen from the train.

About 1 mile from Leigh (pronounced 'lie') the railway and the Medway are crossed by the A21 on a long impressive viaduct. Continuing on through a small wood, we arrive at **Leigh** (formerly Leigh Halt), which is an attractive small village. The village centre is a short walk on the north side of the railway, so turn right into the minor road that passes below the railway. The pub on the green has a tasty array of sandwiches.

The second, and more easterly, southern side road (a cul-de-sac) off the green, leads to a footpath which starts off under a railway bridge, then later crosses the Medway and follows the valley back to Tonbridge. Soon after skirting a lake and passing under the A21 viaduct, the footpath has an early 1980s diversion (so beware of old maps) to take it left, back under the railway, and across a modern concrete footbridge over the Medway just downstream of the new barrage. It then becomes a pleasant riverside walk into Tonbridge.

On leaving Leigh we soon enter a cutting and after passing through a short tunnel we enter **Penshurst** Station – which is actually situated in the village of Chiddingstone Causeway. It is believed that the station is called Penshurst due to its proximity to Penshurst Place. To reach Penshurst Place (about 2 miles distant) either by foot or bicycle, leave the station by the exit which leads to the village. On reaching the main road, turn right and then take the next turning on the right (the B2176) and follow this road to the house. Penshurst Place is also served by Maidstone and District Buses Nos 231 and 233, which run roughly hourly from the station on weekdays and continue the other way to both Edenbridge stations.

The oldest parts of Penshurst Place date back to 1340 and since 1552 the house has been the home of the Sidney family, who have carried the title of Lord De L'Isle since the mid nineteenth century. At the heart of Penshurst Place is the manor, which is dominated by the great hall of 1340 – an outstanding and unique example of medieval architecture. The Queen Elizabeth Room and the Tapestry Room built in the early fifteenth century still retain their Gothic character. Penshurst Place is open every Tuesday to Sunday afternoon from 1 April to the first Sunday in October. Any enquiries should be made to the Administrator – telephone Penshurst (0892) 870307.

**Penshurst** is also the nearest station to the most attractive village of Chiddingstone, which is quite separate from Chiddingstone Causeway. To reach the village, turn left out of the station and follow the Four Elms road (the B2027). Take the first turning on the left and bear right at the next road junction for Chiddingstone. The village contains a number of sixteenth- and seventeenth-century timber-framed houses (some of which are owned by the National Trust) and a seventeenth-century Gothic-style mock castle which is open to the public. Telephone Penshurst 870347 for details.

From Penshurst to Edenbridge the train normally travels at the line-maximum speed, passing through the village of Bough Beech on its way. There have been various moves to have a halt built here to serve the village and Bough Beech Reservoir – a popular spot for walks and picnics which is also used extensively for water-sports.

Edenbridge, the largest intermediate town on the line, has another station, Edenbridge Town on the Uckfield line. **Edenbridge** Station is about fifteen minutes' walk from the town centre, which can be reached by turning right out of the station on to Station Road. For further details of Edenbridge and services on the Uckfield line see Chapter 3.

Shortly after leaving Edenbridge, the line crosses the Uckfield line and then later the East Grinstead–London line. The Tonbridge–Redhill and East Grinstead lines were once linked by a connecting line known as the 'Crowhurst Spur'.

The line has now crossed from Kent into Surrey. We pass through **Godstone** Station, which is situated in South Godstone, Godstone itself lying several miles to the north. The station provides a good starting-point for walks in this largely undiscovered area. Between Godstone and Nutfield we pass through Bletchingley Tunnel and the line is crossed on a viaduct by the M23 Motorway.

**Nutfield** Station is situated in South Nutfield and is the nearest station for Redhill Aerodrome and Heliport, and Nutfield Priory Lake. Leave the station by the path leading from the Redhill platform. Turn right at the end of this path, and then left for the aerodrome, and right for Priory Lake. Redhill Aerodrome is used mostly by light aircraft and is the Head Office of the well-known Bristow Helicopter Group, which operates helicopters in many parts of the world. A Tiger Moth Club is also based here and an annual air show is held every summer. Nutfield Priory Lake is a popular spot for anglers.

Nutfield Station is also quite close to the village of Bletchingley, whose beauty lies in its ancient houses. Timber-framed buildings vie for pride of place with brick and tile-hung houses, where flights of stone steps lead up to wooden front doors. You can reach Bletchingley either by following the road north to the A25 at Nutfield and then turning right (about 2 miles), or by taking one of the footpaths running east from the road a little north of the station. The latter is more pleasant and slightly shorter, but you will need to consult the local Ordnance Survey map.

We continue on to **Redhill** where, after crossing the London–Brighton mainline, we draw into Platform 1 or 2.

# 5

# HAYWARDS HEATH–LEWES–SEAFORD
## by H. Trevor Jones

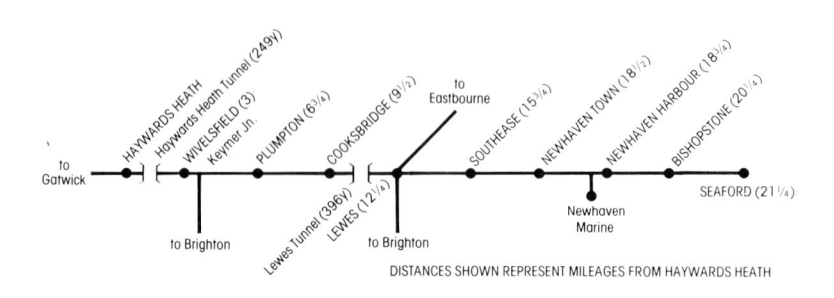

DISTANCES SHOWN REPRESENT MILEAGES FROM HAYWARDS HEATH

Lewes Station, looking up to Lewes Castle on the hill above (Photo: H. Trevor Jones)

Departing from **Haywards Heath** for Lewes and Eastbourne, the train follows the Brighton mainline (see Chapter 1) until the minor station of **Wivelsfield** (a suburb of Burgess Hill) where the train has to slow down and turn sharp left at Keymer Junction for Lewes. Once out of the built-up area and through a cutting, the train passes along an embankment giving a good view on a clear day towards the north-facing escarpment of the South Downs. In particular the two Clayton windmills, nicknamed 'Jack and Jill' (see Chapter 1) can be seen on top of the Downs, by looking a little backwards to the right.

The highest point in the vicinity, in fact directly to your right at this point, is Ditchling Beacon, one of many high points around the South Coast where preparations were made to light a big bonfire to spread the word of the arrival of hostile naval forces in the Channel before the days of radio and telegraph. The energetic can take in its splendid views by walking the South Downs Way along the top of the escarpment, but there is no easy access by public transport.

The next two stations are Plumpton and Cooksbridge, but these are served only by a few Monday-to-Friday peak trains. On the right-hand side of the railway at **Plumpton** Station is the racecourse, meanwhile the village of Plumpton Green on the left-hand side has a pleasant tree-lined village street.

Beyond **Cooksbridge** the line drops down into the Ouse Valley (the Sussex Ouse – not to be confused with several other English rivers bearing the same name), whose upper reaches you probably crossed on that fine viaduct north of Haywards Heath on the Brighton mainline (see Chapter 1). You may just make out on the left (near the village of Hamsey) some earthworks marking the original route of the line coming in from East Grinstead, part of which is now the preserved Bluebell Railway (see Chapter 2), and also from Uckfield; there is just an outside chance that the line from Uckfield will be reinstated in the near future (see also Chapter 3).

After travelling for about a mile almost on top of the right bank of the Ouse, which is tidal at this point, the train passes through a short tunnel under a spur of land on which lies the ancient market town of **Lewes**, and then promptly comes to rest in its station, since, with rare exceptions, all trains call here.

Lewes was an important town even before the Norman Conquest of 1066; it appears at some time to have taken over from Chichester as the seat of government of the former independent Kingdom of Sussex. So it was natural that the Rape of Lewes, one of six divisions of the county of Sussex, was given to one of William the Conqueror's most distinguished followers, de Warenne, who erected Lewes Castle on the hill, situated almost over the railway tunnel, and made it his chief residence. The castle is unusual in possessing two artificial mounds. Besides the Norman remains, there is also a fine fourteenth-century barbican, that is the outer gatehouse. But even if neither of these attractions is of interest to you, the castle (open all year, for details telephone Lewes 474379) is well worth a visit for its fine views over Lewes and up and down the Ouse Valley.

To reach the town centre and castle from the station, turn right out of the station exit into Station Road (which becomes Station Street) and continue ahead up a steep hill to a central crossroads in the main east–west street through the town, now bypassed to the south for through traffic. On the right, School Hill drops down again steeply to the old bridge over the Ouse, but for the castle turn left into the ancient High Street and then right into a side street leading up to the castle entrance. There are many picturesque buildings in the main street, including the so-called Anne of Cleve's House where she is said to have resided after her divorce from Henry VIII.

To reach the bus station, a ten- to fifteen-minute walk from the railway, you can avoid the Station Street hill by turning right into Lansdown Friars and keeping straight on across the main street at the bottom end of School Hill. The most useful bus service for the rail-travelling visitor is the No. 729 (run jointly by three operators) that comes from Brighton and, in particular, fills for the time being the missing link to Uckfield, before continuing to Tunbridge Wells via Crowborough. This bus runs hourly on weekdays and two-hourly on Sundays; there are also additional local buses on weekdays to Uckfield. Another useful bus is the infrequent No. 123 which passes the railway station on its route through some delightful right-bank villages to Newhaven, complementing the railway along the almost deserted left bank.

**Lewes** Station has two platforms served by trains to and from Haywards Heath and London, and three quite separate platforms used by trains to and from Brighton on the East Coastway route, which is joined at Lewes. The station entrance is between the two sets of platforms. Eastbourne and Hastings are served by trains from London, often with good connections into and out of trains from Brighton to Seaford; and there are also through East Coastway trains from Brighton, so check which is due next. There is a buffet on the London-bound platform.

The branch line to Seaford uses the same tracks as the main East Coastway route to Eastbourne for the first mile. *En route* it crosses the River Ouse and cuts through a spur of the hills. After leaving the mainline at Southerham Junction, it follows the left bank of the widening River Ouse to Newhaven, often giving good views across the river to the right. The only intermediate station in the valley is the unstaffed halt that serves the village of **Southease** ½ mile across the valley, together with the larger more distant village of Rodmell.

But Southease is, however, a good station for ramblers, as this is where the South Downs Way long-distance footpath (see also Chapter 6) crosses the River Ouse. The walk eastwards from here follows the top of the escarpment to the picturesque village of Alfriston (see below) in the Cuckmere Valley, then onwards to Eastbourne and Beachy Head, giving good views northwards towards the Wealden ridges on a clear day. There are also frequent views down the gentle slopes towards the sea, which lies up to 4 miles to the south.

On reaching **Newhaven** the branch trains first serve Newhaven Town Station and then, a minute later, Newhaven Harbour Station, before continuing to Seaford. Special through boat trains from London, connecting with sailings to Dieppe in France, serve a separate platform within the harbour confines, effectively making a third station for this small town.

From Newhaven Town Station, it is a short walk across the river to the right of the train and then straight on to reach the town centre. But the most interesting attraction for visitors to the town is Fort Newhaven, which is situated on the headland on the town-centre side of the river. To reach the fort, turn left immediately after crossing the river and continue for a mile along a road that gives good views of all the activity in the harbour.

At the end of the road, where it curves round the foot of the headland beneath the fort, are a few seaside amusements and places of refreshment. At low tide there is also a small beach protected by the main harbour breakwater, from the end of which there are good views eastwards to Seaford Head and back inland to the Downs.

On the inland side of the fort there is the beginning of a coastal footpath over the headland to Peacehaven, which then continues onwards along the built-up cliff-top until it joins the main coast road at Saltdean. Along this road runs the half-hourly (hourly on Sundays) No. 712 bus from Eastbourne to Brighton via Seaford and Newhaven. On the cliff-top in the middle of Peacehaven is an obelisk marking the Meridian of Greenwich (namely 0 degrees longitude), on which the village of Peacehaven was symbolically constructed.

But back in the train any view of the harbour is hidden by the port buildings. After the Harbour Station the railway becomes single track and passes the suburban station of **Bishopstone** before terminating in the centre of **Seaford**, only a short walk from the town's shingle beach. The original village of Bishopstone, mentioned in 'Domesday Book', having a church with a Norman chancel, is up on the Downs almost a mile inland from Bishopstone Station. But on the sea-front in Seaford itself is one of the chain of Martello towers running all round the south-east coast as part of its defences in Napoleonic times; this one has been converted into a local museum which is open all year (for details telephone Seaford 898222).

At Seaford the main bus routes go right past the station. Besides the No. 712 mentioned above, there is also a weekdays-only, two-hourly No. 126 bus to Eastbourne the long way round via Alfriston, Berwick, and Polegate. The first leg of this bus ride is well worth taking, both for the excellent view over the unspoilt Cuckmere Valley from a point called 'High and Over', and then for the exquisite delights of the picturesque village of Alfriston. The village has a good selection of quaint tea-houses in its narrow main street and its church actually backs on to the Cuckmere River, the haunt of swans and other wildfowl. From Alfriston the keen walker can take the South Downs Way (see above) in either direction, or can walk down a path along the banks of the Cuckmere back to the main coast road at Exceat Bridge (see below).

At the far end of Seaford's sea-front, there is a pathway which starts quite steeply up Seaford Head, becoming more gentle towards the top. On the top are the earthworks of an ancient fort, which affords good coastal views back to Fort Newhaven on its lower headland, and on to Brighton in the distance. But the best is yet to come, for about a mile farther on, with the pathway still pretty high up, comes what this chapter's writer considers the most beautiful coastal view in south-east England – that of the Seven Sisters, an undulating line of cliffs with seven brows, from Seaford Head, looking across Cuckmere Haven, the only unspoilt river estuary in south-east England. If you are very lucky, you might be able to ford the river on the beach at low tide, but otherwise, short of returning to Seaford, the pathway must be followed inland up the valley the mile or so to Exceat Bridge where the main road, with its No. 712 bus, crosses the river.

On the main road, on the other, east, side of the valley, about ¼ mile and one bus stop from the bridge, in a converted eighteenth-century barn, is the Interpretative Centre for the Seven Sisters Country Park. The park lies within the Sussex Heritage Coast, which has been recognised by the Countryside Commission as 'one of the few remaining unspoilt stretches of coast of outstanding scenic value in England and Wales' – according to the cheap but useful little booklet entitled *Seven Sisters Park*

*Trail* that you can buy there. The centre is a mine of information on all the different natural animal, vegetable, and mineral features of this area of downland. Across the road is the bend of one of the former meanders of the River Cuckmere, now a pleasant little backwater popular with wildfowl since a direct channel was cut in 1846 to facilitate navigation up to Alfriston. These meanders are one of the many large-scale attractive features of the landscape of the valley when it is viewed from the downland hills on either side, or, if preferred, from the top deck of a bus.

The Park Trail takes the walker back to the sea down the left bank of the Cuckmere Valley; there is, in fact, a choice of possible paths. From the shingle beach of Cuckmere Haven, it is an exhilarating cliff-top walk of about 2 miles over the Seven Sisters to Birling Gap, and then a further couple of miles up to Beachy Head and down to the outskirts of Eastbourne. The seven ups and downs are no more than moderately steep, that is, it is walking rather than scrambling, and the coastal views of the white chalk cliffs are superb all the way, not forgetting to look behind you at intervals to see the view back to Seaford Head. The first 'Sister', Haven Brow, is actually the highest, higher even than Seaford Head if you deviate slightly inland to its triangulation point, where there are good views back to Brighton and even as far as the low headland of Selsey Bill, 40 miles to the west, on a very clear day. Birling Gap is the lowest point in between Cuckmere Haven and Eastbourne, yet even here it has been necessary to construct scaffolding steps in order to provide the only intermediate access to the sea. A cliff-top hotel by the steps can provide an open-air afternoon tea, a welcome break for the long-distance walker.

Those who are getting tired can walk 1½ miles inland along the road to East Dean, on the main east–west road, to catch the No. 712 bus or, on summer Sundays only, catch a very occasional bus travelling via Birling Gap and Beachy Head. But otherwise you now have a choice between taking the road or the cliff-top path to Beachy Head, where there is a pub/restaurant with a view. The bright red lighthouse can also be seen on the rocks or in the sea below, according to the tide. The writer's calculations suggest that that top of the Isle of Wight hills, about 60 miles away, can theoretically be seen above the horizon from Beachy Head, but he has never been able to confirm this himself. But now, being on the main headland, nearly 540 feet above sea-level and marking the end of the South Downs, there is also an extensive view eastwards across Eastbourne and Pevensey Bay to the Wealden sandstone cliffs beyond Hastings 15 miles away. From Beachy Head to Eastbourne, there is a choice between a path dropping at first very steeply at right angles to the road, just past the end of the sheer chalk cliffs at Beachy Head, or a gentler shorter path leaving the road at an angle a little farther on – or, in summer only, you can catch an Eastbourne town bus. (See Chapter 6 for further information about Eastbourne.)

# 6

## BRIGHTON–LEWES–EASTBOURNE–HASTINGS
### by H. Trevor Jones

The East Coastway line from Brighton curves sharp right across a high viaduct over the town very soon after leaving Brighton Station (see Chapter 1), giving quite a good view; the right-hand side is the most interesting, where the sea can be seen in the distance. The first two stations, **Brighton London Road** and **Moulsecoomb**,

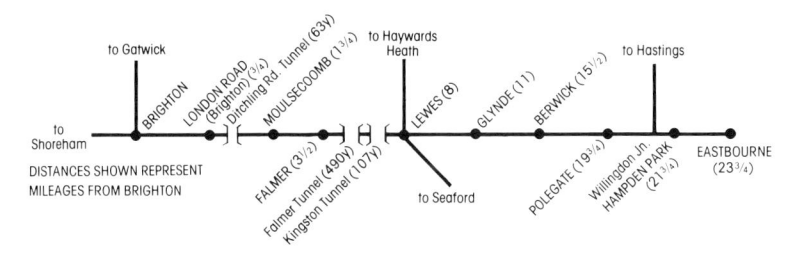

```
to Gatwick          to Haywards
                     Heath                         to Hastings
   BRIGHTON  LONDON ROAD (¾)        LEWES (8)  GLYNDE (11)  BERWICK (15½)
             (Brighton) (¾)  MOULSECOOMB (1¾)
to           Ditchling Rd. Tunnel (6¾)                                    EASTBOURNE
Shoreham     FALMER (3½)                         POLEGATE (19¾)           (23¾)
DISTANCES SHOWN REPRESENT  Falmer Tunnel (490y)                Willingdon Jn
MILEAGES FROM BRIGHTON     Kingston Tunnel (107y)    to Seaford    HAMPDEN PARK (21½)
```

are in the suburbs of Brighton up a valley to the north-east followed by both the railway and the main eastbound trunk road. Moulescoomb was opened in May 1980, the first completly new Southern Region station since the Beeching era.

The next and only other station before Lewes is **Falmer**, built to serve a little village almost on top of the railway tunnel that follows. But to the immediate right of the station, just outside the built-up conurbation of modern Brighton, is a technical college, and, of greater national importance, across the main road to the immediate left of the railway, is the campus of the University of Sussex. Because of the proximity of the main road, this is also the most convenient interchange point for the No. 729 bus to Uckfield and Tunbridge Wells (see Chapter 5 for details) as this bus serves Brighton Station no better than Lewes Station and almost all trains call at Falmer.

Beyond the tunnel the train, now travelling almost due east, drops down a pleasant green valley to Lewes (see Chapter 5), affording good views of the downland scenery on each side once a cutting is left behind.

After leaving Lewes, the railway to Eastbourne remains to the north of the South Downs, except for the first little bit to **Glynde** where it leaves the Ouse Valley and follows a tributary upstream as it cuts back through the Downs. Another pleasant walk, less well known than the coastal walks, is a direct path over the hill between Lewes and Glynde. At nearby Glyndebourne lies the world-famous opera-house converted out of a large country house in an attractive rural setting, so if a dinner-jacketed gentleman alights from the train at Glynde, that is probably where he is going!

From here, all the way to Eastbourne, there are good views of the northern scarp of the South Downs to the right of the train. The next station is **Berwick**, which is over a mile from its village – not to be confused with Berwick-on-Tweed in Northumberland. Then comes **Polegate**, marking the northern outskirts of the Eastbourne conurbation. Buses from Eastbourne to Hailsham and beyond (see below) pass over the level crossing by the recently resited station. The earthworks of the former direct line to Hastings are still clearly visible, bypassing the now necessary deviation by all trains into Eastbourne. This is probably the only place in the country where you can just miss catching an express train travelling from London, jump into a local bus, and catch the train up a few stations later, namely at Westham!

**Hampden Park**, a lesser suburb of Eastbourne and the last intermediate station, is where the line from Hastings joins that from Lewes into a common trunk to Eastbourne. There is a long-term proposal to develop the marshlands between here and Eastbourne proper into a large mixed leisure area, with a small amount of light industry thrown in.

At **Eastbourne** the station is one of the more attractive of those serving the South Coast resorts, with an architecturally interesting clock-tower in one corner of the buildings. The concourse inside has recently been modernised, and as well as a smart Travellers Fare buffet, there is a licensed restaurant called 'The Inn on the Track' doing rather more exotic meals at quite reasonable prices, which can be recommended. Turn left out of the station and then keep straight on to pass through the main shopping centre and eventually reach the sea.

On the way, only a few hundred yards from the station, you pass through a street for buses only, where all the principal routes have a stop. The stops for the No. 126 to Seaford via Alfriston (see Chapter 5) and for the No. 712 to Seaford, Newhaven, and Brighton are both on the far side near the far end of this section of road. A recommended country excursion is to take the No. 712 to the Seven Sisters Park Centre at Exceat and then walk back along the coast, as described in Chapter 5. A shorter excursion just to visit Beachy Head, especially off-season when there are no local town buses there, is to take this same bus just to the top of the Downs scarp, by a golf-course, and then walk leftwards out to Beachy Head along the South Downs Way. Another interesting trip is on the No. 98 bus, which journeys inland along a scenic route via Hailsham and Herstmonceux before returning to the seaside at Bexhill and ending at Ore, the far side of Hastings, two hours later. For details of Eastbourne to Uckfield buses, see Chapter 3.

The old part of Eastbourne is actually half-way up the hill on the main road to Seaford. The present town centre, in the words of *The 1066 Country* guide-book, 'owes its gracious charm to the seventh Duke of Devonshire who conceived a Victorian development in "the grandest manner". Tree-lined avenues, attractive parks and the famous floral gardens, along the sea-front, all enhance this sunny town.' Beachy Head does provide some protection from approaching inclement weather. The Duke imposed a condition that there be no shops along the sea-front, which is thus very carefully controlled to avoid the sort of commercial development associated with most South Coast sea-front promenades.

Indeed the town can be said to be more up-market than its rival Hastings, but lacking the latter's old-world charm. The promenade, from the pier for almost 2 miles to the foot of Beachy Head, is really quite an attractive and fairly peaceful walk, especially at the farther end where the adjacent road has disappeared some way above, on top of a small preliminary cliff. At the bandstand on the promenade is a display of detailed weather information. Eastbourne is also a good place for pleasurable activities, from theatres to the children's Treasure Island play centre a little way to the east of the pier – worth taking a bus from the station if you have small children.

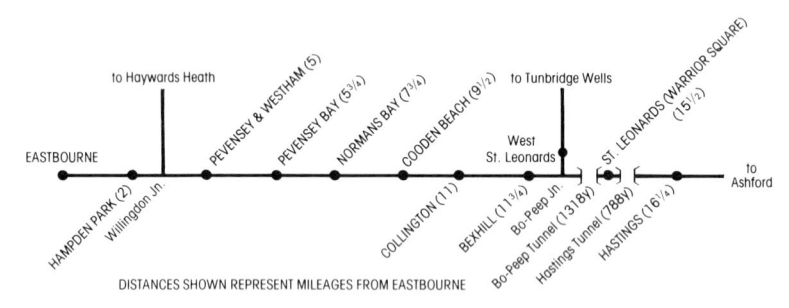

DISTANCES SHOWN REPRESENT MILEAGES FROM EASTBOURNE

If the passenger remains in the train at Eastbourne, he will reverse direction and retraverse the route back to Hampden Park before branching off towards the next station, **Pevensey & Westham**, actually in the village of Westham, and at which all trains call. Then less than a mile farther on is the unstaffed halt called **Pevensey Bay**, served only by stopping trains, which is actually nearer the old village of Pevensey and is ½ mile from the modern seaside resort of Pevensey Bay.

But the principal attraction in this vicinity is Pevensey Castle, which lies immediately to the north on the left-hand side of the railway, half-way between the two stations, and is now mostly in ruins. It is a Norman castle, built within Roman walls and moated. This is where the conquering Normans landed from France in 1066. One of the first things they did was to build, in 1080, the adjacent Church of St Mary the Virgin in Westham, where three of the original windows and a chapel remain, the rest being thirteenth- and fifteenth-century work. The best view, of church and castle together, is from the footpath going south over the railway, across the water-meadows which were sea when the Normans first came. Also at Pevensey, in the old village street at the east end of the castle, is 'The Ancient Mint House circa AD 1342' which invites the visitor to see 'where coins were minted in AD 1076', as well as fourteenth-century carvings and frescos.

Beyond Pevensey Bay comes **Normans Bay**, another unstaffed halt, serving a group of holiday caravans on the coast at a location traditionally considered by some to be the Norman landing site; but there is not much to see here, although there is quite a good pub rather off the beaten track. Then comes **Cooden Beach**, which is the station nearest the sea and is served by fast trains. It marks the start of the Bexhill built-up area, which, along the main road, is continuous into St Leonards and Hastings. Just before the station is a good sea-view looking right back to Beachy Head. Meanwhile some distance out to sea lies the modern concrete Royal Sovereign light platform, which has a helicopter landing-pad perched on stilts above the water. The present light platform replaced the former staffed lightship.

The suburban halt of **Collington** comes next, before **Bexhill** Station is reached. Here, between railway and sea-front, is a small modern shopping centre, although the town's original centre stood on a hill to the north. In the Old Town there is an interesting Costume Museum; and along the promenade there are the usual seaside amusements. Most of the town was in the hands of the De la Warr family, and until recently there were no pubs between the railway and the sea. The wide platforms on the station were built to accommodate the large pre-war crowds of schoolchildren, coming to several private boarding-schools, who would clutter the place with their luggage that had to last a whole school term.

At the west end of Bexhill sea-front there is a nice restaurant in the De la Warr Pavilion. The east end peters out into a pleasant low cliff walk over Galley Hill to Glyne Gap, where you can either cut inland under the main road to catch a bus, or you can continue along the shingle shore beside the railway to St Leonards. Indeed, at spring high tide the sea is pretty close, both horizontally and vertically, to the railway; but at low tide fascinating pools and streams can be seen in gently shelving fine, and occasionally muddy, sand. Here also is the protected site of an ancient shipwreck, uncovered only at exceptionally low tides.

Eastbourne

Back in the train, after passing this sea-view to the right and carriage sidings to the left (an odd combination), the train turns slightly inland, and joins the direct line from London to Hastings via Tunbridge Wells (described in *KESR*), at the quaintly named 'Bopeep Junction' (not a station). Then after a long tunnel comes **St Leonards** Station at Warrior Square, serving an even smaller seaside shopping centre than Bexhill, together with several hotels. It is here that passengers have to leave the station, ascend a footbridge, and return on the other side in order to change trains for Battle and Tunbridge Wells. Many buildings in St Leonards were designed by Decimus Burton and are now listed for their architectural value – the Royal Victoria Hotel is a good example.

Finally another, shorter, tunnel takes the train to **Hastings** Station, which is the principal station of the conurbation and where most trains from all directions terminate. The principal attractions in Hastings (which are described in much greater detail in *KESR*) are, going from west to east: the pier and adjacent White Rock Gardens, the modern main shopping centre and most hotels lying not far from the station, the castle and caves on Castle Hill, the old town and the fishing harbour with its unique black wooden 'shops' for hanging nets to dry, and lastly the spectacular high cliff walks from the East Cliff towards Fairlight. Hastings is also the place to change trains for the ancient and picturesque town of Rye, on the cross-country route to Ashford (described in *KESR*). The main terminal for buses is in the forecourt just outside the station, but buses on some routes have to be caught down the hill in the town centre five minutes' walk away.

# 7

# LONDON VICTORIA–SUTTON–HORSHAM
## by I. McGill

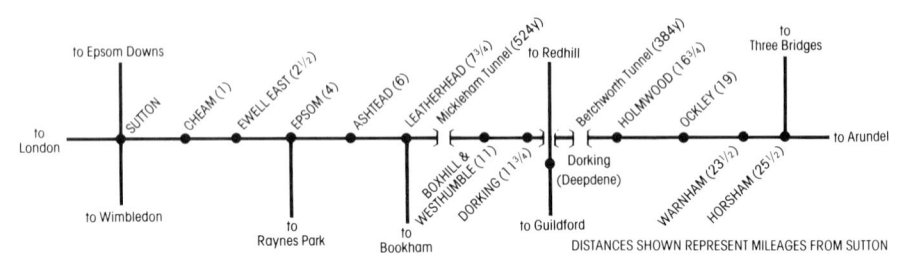

From **Victoria** to **Balham**, we follow the Brighton mainline (see Chapter 1 for details). After Balham Junction the train crosses Tooting Common and negotiates Streatham Junction, to head south. Mitcham Common is an oasis amid the urban dreariness, as the train slows down to negotiate the sharp curves at **Mitcham Junction**, whose platforms are also used by the two-coach trains providing a local service over the curious little line between Wimbledon and West Croydon. Journeying through the leafy suburbs at **Hackbridge** and **Carshalton**, the train continues towards **Sutton**, where a line from West Croydon converges on the left.

Sutton was once a Surrey village on the London to Brighton turnpike. However, following the coming of the railway in 1847, it soon became engulfed by the southern sprawl of suburbia, and is now the thriving administrative centre of the London borough to which it gave its name in 1965.

The station is just south of the town centre, and buses on several routes conveniently call at or near the entrance in Brighton Road. Sutton is well served by the frequent EMUs of the Southern Region's extensive suburban network, and is the junction for the Epsom Downs branch. Trains to Dorking and beyond leave from Platform 2, and follow the route once used by mainline trains to the West Sussex coast, until these were diverted to run via East Croydon and Gatwick Airport in May 1978. The Wimbledon line can be seen descending sharply beyond the platforms, before veering off to the right. This steeply graded line was planned specifically for electric traction and was opened by the Southern Railway in 1930, to serve an area which was extensively developed between the two world wars.

The built-up area continues until, at **Cheam**, open spaces begin to mingle with the expansive gardens of outer suburbia. Nonsuch Park, a remnant of the great estate which surrounded Henry VIII's opulent but vanished Nonsuch Palace, is glimpsed distantly to the right, as the train nears **Ewell**, whose estates soon merge imperceptibly with Epsom. Just before reaching the junction with the former LSWR line from Waterloo via Raynes Park, a low, slate-roofed building of greying brick can be seen on the left. This is the former Epsom Town Station, where trains from Sutton terminated until the line was extended through to Leatherhead in 1859. **Epsom**'s present spacious four-platform station was built by the Southern Railway in the late 1920s and is conveniently situated for the High Street.

Despite its proximity to London, Epsom retains something of its character as a country market town, and is a good starting-point for walks across the Downs with their famous racecourse, or over the extensive commons to Ashtead, where the train can be rejoined. Prosperity was assured for Epsom when it became a resort of Society, following the discovery, in 1618, of medicinal springs whose waters were impregnated with what we now know as Epsom Salts. The original well is about a mile from the station, and lies almost forgotten in a corner of the modern Wells estate. The town centre retains some features of interest, and there is a bustling Saturday market which complements the modern Ashley shopping centre. The visitor seeking refreshment has a splendid choice of hostelries, and there is even a theatre – the Epsom Playhouse.

The area between Epsom and Leatherhead gives the impression of being in the front line of battle between town and country. However, at **Ashtead**, the wide expanse of common which stretches away to the right still bravely holds out against the advancing tide of bricks and mortar, which continues almost unabated on the opposite side of the railway. After passing under two new bridges carrying the M25 and the Leatherhead bypass, the line curves to the left before reaching **Leatherhead**.

This country town grew up round a river crossing, where the Mole breaks through the North Downs to enter the Surrey Plain, and is a good centre for exploring the surrounding area, especially the Mickleham Valley and North Downs, which lie just south of the town. An especially attractive ramble takes one through Norbury Park and Druids Grove, along the wooden western flank of the Mickleham Valley, descending to reach the railway at Boxhill Station. However, there are many other alternatives to be found with the aid of a good map. For the less energetic, Leatherhead has an interesting museum (although opening hours are restricted), while a nearby water park makes a good venue for a family outing; or you may prefer simply to wander around the pedestrian shopping precinct, relax by the river, or be entertained at the Thorndike Theatre.

Parting company with the line to Bookham and Effingham Junction (described in Chapter 11), the train crosses the River Mole and leaving Leatherhead behind, burrows beneath Norbury Park by means of the 524-yard-long Mickleham Tunnel. It emerges in the Mickleham Valley, with wooded slopes on either hand and the Mole meandering lazily, as though loathe to leave this well-timbered vale. There is a

An Epsom-bound train enters Boxhill & Westhumble Station, which still retains its attractive downside buildings (Photo: Graham Collett)

glimpse of Mickleham village on the left nestling hard against the lower slopes of the North Downs, before approaching **Boxhill & Westhumble** Station, which lies virtually in the shadow of Box Hill, whose slopes rise to a height of over 600 feet.

Box Hill is said to derive its name from the once-profuse growth of box trees, but nowadays the predominant species are probably yew and juniper. A mere 500-yard walk from the station (taking care to cross the busy A24 by the subway provided) will bring you to the foot of this popular beauty-spot, near the Burford Bridge Hotel, from where the steep ascent may be attempted by one of several routes. Or, if you are feeling more adventurous, you may turn left over the railway bridge, that is away from Box Hill, walk along Chapel Lane and through West Humble village, to reach a network of tracks and bridleways which will take you over the breezy heights of Ranmore and down towards Dorking, or to the magnificent house and grounds at Polesden Lacey – owned by the National Trust. The gardens are open all year, and the house from March to October (for current opening times and charges telephone Bookham 58203), and there is also an open-air theatre in summer.

Nearer the station, in Chapel Lane, are the remains of the late twelfth-century West Humble Chapel, also in the care of the National Trust. The area is rich in historic and literary associations. The Queen Mother spent her honeymoon at Polesden Lacey and the Burford Bridge Hotel has numbered among its guests Keats, R. L. Stevenson, and Lord Nelson.

The Valley of the Mole broadens perceptibly as the train heads south to arrive in about a mile at **Dorking** (formerly **Dorking North**) Station, where most trains now terminate. Electric trains first reached Dorking in 1925, when the service from Waterloo via Raynes Park commenced; this was followed in 1929 by the introduction of electric services from London Bridge. Then in 1938 electrification was extended to Horsham and beyond.

You will probably arrive at Platform 2 or 3, and have to negotiate the narrow subway to reach the booking-hall and exit on Platform 1. Modern facilities, which represent a great improvement for customers and staff alike, have recently been provided at this station, in conjunction with a commercial development. For the town centre, cross the A24 dual carriageway by the subway at the end of the station approach, and passing beneath the Guildford–Redhill line, continue until you reach a roundabout and then turn right into Reigate Road.

On summer Sundays and Bank Holidays, Ramblers Bus No. 417 leaves from outside the station. It will take you on a tour through some of the magnificent countryside which lies to the west of Dorking, and to the villages around Leith Hill which are otherwise inaccessible by public transport (telephone Dorking 882281 for times and fares). For further information about Dorking see Chapter 10.

Returning to Dorking Station, trains to Horsham depart from the island platform at about two-hourly intervals during off-peak hours and more frequently during peak periods. However, there is no Sunday service south of Dorking.

Immediately after leaving Dorking, the train passes beneath the Guildford–Redhill line (described in Chapter 10). The A25 passes above, and the train quickly reaches Betchworth Tunnel, to emerge after 384 yards into open country, where the lingering threat of suburbia seems finally to have been vanquished.

Looking back, the bare southern slopes of Box Hill are seen to contrast markedly with its wooded western flank and the heavily timbered escarpment of the North Downs farther west. There are wide views to the left along the Vale of Holmesdale, while the spire of Brockham Church is prominent across the fields. More often known as Brockham Green, this village stages spectacular Bonfire Night celebrations each 5 November, and every third summer a 'medieval fayre' is held here. With cottages picturesquely scattered round a spacious green, and benignly presided over by the large church, it is well worth a visit and can easily be reached by bus from Dorking.

Abinger Forest and the wooded heights around Leith Hill (see Chapter 10) gain prominence on the right, beyond Holmwood Common, as the railway describes a long, lazy arc south-westwards passing a sub-station on the right before reaching **Holmwood**, some 5 miles from Dorking. Although off-peak trains call here, they do not stop at the other intermediate stations – **Ockley** and **Warnham**.

Holmwood serves a rural and predominantly scattered catchment area; the nearest settlement is at Beare Green, about ¾ mile to the south. It does, however, provide an excellent starting-point for ramblers, being the nearest station to Leith Hill and the breezy heights around Coldharbour.

Leaving Holmwood, the rolling Surrey countryside stretches away on either side. A large and impressive house, which is seen to the right on a ridge of high ground, is Trouts Farm, beyond which the railway is spanned by a bridge carrying the main London to Bognor road. The rural tranquillity is soon intruded upon by a close encounter with the Capel bypass, which flirts briefly with the railway before sweeping back, like a recalcitrant child, to rejoin its parent, the A24. The vista of a peaceful pastoral landscape is restored once more, punctuated only by the fleeting glimpse of a rectifier sub-station on the right as the train hurries on its way.

There is not a habitation in sight as the train approaches **Ockley** (formerly **Ockley and Capel**) Station, which stands solitary and remote from the villages it purports to serve, amid the lush green acres of this lonely rural corner of Surrey. The station buildings are neat and trim and remain virtually complete, with a dainty little awning which projects out over the down platform from the station house. Strangely, there has been no post-railway development here, as has often occurred elsewhere, and the railway is, anyway, such an unobtrusive feature of the landscape at this point that, approaching by road, one is liable to come upon the station with some surprise.

Of the adjacent villages, Capel is the nearest, lying about a mile to the east, while Ockley is about 1½ miles to the west. Ockley is a somewhat scattered Wealden village strung out along the line of the old Roman Stane Street, its lovely time-mellowed buildings mostly clustered round an extensive green. The shortest route between the station and the village is to turn right at the end of the station approach road, beneath the railway bridge into Coles Lane and in about 500 yards turn left along a signposted bridle-path, through the woods, to eventually emerge just south of the village green. However, in so doing, one misses the church (which contains work of

35

various periods from the fourteenth to the nineteenth centuries), situated farther along Coles Lane on the right, opposite Ockley Court and a farm shop.

The character of the landscape remains largely unchanged for a further mile or two until the extensive works of the former Sussex Brick Company appear on the left; the company used the deposits of Wealden Clay as their raw material. The county boundary between Surrey and West Sussex is crossed hereabouts, as the line swings through a series of curves to pass another sub-station near **Warnham**,* where there is a gated level crossing. Near by is Warnham Court with its deer park, and Field Place, where the poet Percy Bysshe Shelley was born on 4 August 1792.

Boldings Brook, which has been keeping company with the railway for about a mile, remains close by until the prevailing woodland gradually yields to the outskirts of Horsham. A formidable complex of industrial buildings looms on the left and extensive sidings fan out to the right. In a few seconds, the line from Three Bridges (described in Chapter 8) sweeps in from the left, and the train runs into one of **Horsham**'s four platforms.

Horsham is a market town which well repays a visit. Turn left from the station into North Street, and you will eventually arrive at the Carfax, in the town centre, with its delicate cast-iron bandstand shaded by trees. This is also where the main bus stops are situated. Near by are The Causeway and Pump Alley, probably the most picturesque parts of the town, but there are also a host of individual buildings of interest, including the manor house, the parish church, town hall, and museum. Many buildings are roofed with a characteristic material known as 'Horsham slabs', which are, in effect, large tiles made from a locally quarried stone. Bus and train services radiating from the town make it a good centre from which to explore farther afield. For further information about the town and surrounding area see Chapter 8.

* The Warnham Military Museum (still shown on some maps) has now moved to Eastleigh Airport.

# 8

## GATWICK AIRPORT–CHICHESTER (INCLUDING LITTLEHAMPTON AND BOGNOR REGIS)

### by Simon A. Jeffs

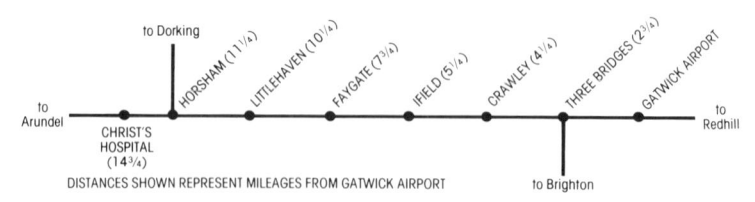

Our journey between Gatwick and Chichester will take us from the bustling atmosphere of an international airport to the quiet of an English cathedral town, passing through one of Britain's largest new towns, the birthplace of the English iron industry, past a riverside castle, desolate marshes, and Victorian seaside resorts.

The historical development of the line divides the route into four sections. The stretch from Gatwick to Three Bridges comprises the first section of the route, and forms that part of the London–Brighton Railway opened in 1841. Next we enter the Mid-Sussex line, opened to Horsham in 1848 and to Midhurst in 1859, which linked the two major market towns of the Sussex Weald with the London–Brighton mainline. The line from Worthing to Chichester was opened in 1846, while the gap between the Mid-Sussex and the coast line was filled in 1863. The branches to Littlehampton and Bognor also date from this time.

From **Gatwick Airport** to **Three Bridges** we follow the Brighton mainline (see Chapter 1 for details). Then curving sharply right, we enter the branch to Horsham and shortly arrive at **Crawley**, where the present station dates from 1968. Crawley expanded as a post-war New Town and now has a population approaching 80,000, but its origins lie in the twelfth century – as is evidenced by the Church of St John. The station is well located for the large shopping centre and bus station.

After leaving Crawley, and passing through the platforms of the original Crawley Station, a short ride brings us to **Ifield**. Ifield, **Littlehaven**, and **Roffey Road Halt** were opened in 1907 as country halts, but whereas the former two have been progressively modernised to meet the needs of their growing traffic, Roffey Road was closed in 1937.

Ifield's long history stretches back at least as far as 'Domesday Book'. It was the site of one of the blast-furnaces which were in operation across the Weald between the late fifteenth and early eighteenth centuries. A description of the Sussex iron-smelting industry is given in Chapter 3.

The next station, **Faygate**, is now only open during peak hours, but it was formerly an important station for goods and agricultural traffic. **Littlehaven**, despite serving the mushrooming Horsham suburbs, retains a rather dilapidated booking-office and wheel-operated level-crossing gates for the perusal of its many passengers. A further short journey brings us to **Horsham**, a town worthy of some attention.

Horsham's first period of prosperity dates from the twelfth century, as is evidenced by the magnificent St Mary's Church at the end of The Causeway – the oldest street in town. The Horsham Museum (telephone 0403 54959) is also to be found here, and gives a good introduction to the town's history. Nowadays, Horsham is a prosperous town which has developed out of all recognition from its original market-town status. Light industry, office development, Gatwick Airport, and a heavy commuter traffic all continue to aid its growth.

This growth was quickly facilitated by the arrival of railways from Three Bridges, Midhurst, Shoreham, Guildford, and Leatherhead between 1848 and 1867. The present station, with its unconventional frontage, dates from the rebuilding of 1938 when the Mid-Sussex line was electrified. As the town centre is a considerable distance from the station, you may wish to fortify yourself before returning – perhaps with a pint of the town's most famous product, King & Barnes ale! Some further information about Horsham is given in Chapter 7.

The line south of Horsham is now marketed as the Arun Valley line and appears in BR's list of scenic rail routes. While passing through the next station on the line, **Christ's Hospital**, the observant traveller may notice that it was once a junction of some size.

Opened in 1902, the station was built to serve the newly relocated Christ's Hospital public school, and an anticipated housing development to be known as 'West Horsham'. Because of these proposed developments, platforms were opened on the Guildford line for the first time, and the station developed into a minor interchange for passengers travelling between the Shoreham and Guildford lines. Alas, West Horsham never materialised, the lines to Guildford and Shoreham closed in the mid 1960s, and the station was 'rationalised' to its present appearance in 1972. Now it only opens for schoolchildren and commuters. Musing on how the mighty have fallen, we head off into the Weald for our next stop, **Billingshurst**.

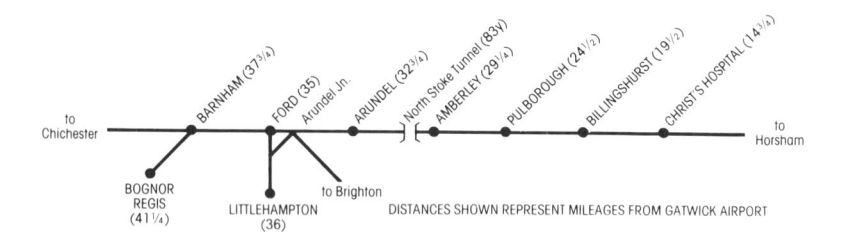

```
                                        BARNHAM (37¾)
                                                FORD (35)
                                                    Arundel Jn.
                                                        ARUNDEL (32¾)
                                                            North Stoke Tunnel (83y)
                                                                AMBERLEY (29¼)
                                                                    PULBOROUGH (24½)
                                                                        BILLINGSHURST (19½)
                                                                            CHRIST'S HOSPITAL (14½)
    to                                                                                              to
Chichester ●────────────●───●───●────●──┤ ├──●────────●───────●─────────────────────●  Horsham
                        │     \ │
                        │      \│
                    BOGNOR      │
                    REGIS      to Brighton
                    (41¼)   LITTLEHAMPTON    DISTANCES SHOWN REPRESENT MILEAGES FROM GATWICK AIRPORT
                              (36)
```

In the sixteenth century, Billingshurst was the centre of the Wealden glass-making industry, and its importance at this time is evidenced by the rebuilding of the parish church and the establishment of a grammar school. Nowadays, it is a small market town with groups of old cottages in its two main streets, pleasant pubs and restaurants, and a small thriving shopping centre. The station building is an unimposing structure, but deserves a place in the history of the town as it had the greatest single effect on its development.

**Pulborough** probably owes its foundation to the Romans and its development to its fortuitous position on Stane Street, one of the principal Roman roads which crosses the River Arun at this point. Numerous Roman relics are associated with Stane Street, the most famous of which is Bignor Roman Villa, which can be reached either by bicycle from Pulborough or Amberley, or by a pleasant 4-mile walk across the Downs from Amberley. Bignor is open from 1 March to 31 October, Tuesday to Sunday – telephone Sutton (07987) 259 for details of opening hours.

By the eleventh century, Pulborough was the centre of extensive Norman hunting-grounds, and a small motte and bailey was erected to supervise them. The area developed further with the coming of the iron industry, the improvement of the Arun (allowing ships to reach the sea at Littlehampton), the building of the Wey & Arun Canal (permitting a through link from the Arun to the Thames), and the opening of the Mid-Sussex line. Pulborough is now a quiet village (but a notorious traffic bottleneck on summer week-ends!) with a healthy (and wealthy) commuter traffic, and is a pleasant place to fish, stroll along the river, or sample the waterside pubs.

After crossing the wide flood plain of the Arun, the Downs loom up before us and we stop at **Amberley**, which is actually in Houghton Bridge; Amberley village, with its thatched cottages and castle, is a stiff 1-mile walk up the hill. Houghton Bridge

A London to Bognor Regis train approaches Amberley Station (Photo: I. McGill)

itself has an excellent hostelry and several riverside cafés but its major attraction is now the Chalk Pits Museum, whose entrance is adjacent to the station.

The museum contains a number of working relics illustrating the industrial history of southern England, including a 2-foot-gauge railway system with several working steam and diesel locomotives, and is located in the former Pepper's chalk-pits and limekilns. The museum, which also has its own refreshment facilities, is usually open from 1 April to 31 October, Wednesday to Sunday and also on Bank Holiday Mondays. For further details telephone Bury (079 881) 370.

The South Downs Way crosses the Arun here, and Amberley can be made the starting-point for several Downland rambles. The station itself, whose closure was averted by the opening of the museum, is a gem of LBSCR architecture, right down to the gleaming signal-cabin on the down platform.

After crossing the Arun twice more, we arrive at **Arundel**. Although the town is dominated by its famous castle, the Anglican church and Roman Catholic cathedral are also prominent on the skyline. The delights of Arundel are described fully below. Once a major riverside port, the coming of the railway led to its decline, and the development of Littlehampton at its expense.

Having passed through one of the most beautiful areas in the south, the Arun Valley line joins the coast line at Arundel Junction. This is a quiet, desolate place, given over to the birds and other wildlife which inhabit the extensive reed marshes bordering the widening Arun. Most trains from Arundel travel on to Bognor Regis, and a change at Ford is necessary to reach Littlehampton. However, we shall go the quick way, and, curving sharply left at Arundel Junction, we enter the Littlehampton branch and shortly arrive at **Littlehampton**, with its station building newly constructed in 1987.

Unlike our Victorian forebears, we can no longer catch a steamer to France, the Channel Islands, or the Isle of Wight, but this loss is amply compensated for by the delights of Littlehampton's beaches. The East beach is a short walk from the station and is the more commercialised, with all the usual seaside amenities and a large amusement park. For a quieter day out, cross the Arun by the footbridge and follow the river to West beach, with its extensive sand-dunes. The broad expanses of perfect sand and the warm, shallow sea make Littlehampton the ideal place for a day out.

Back on the coast line, our train crosses the Arun and arrives at **Ford**, a small village on the west bank of the river. The station has very few local users and remains open as the junction for the Littlehampton branch. The service pattern to Littlehampton is continually changing, and Ford's future may be less secure than the inhabitants of HM Prison, Ford!

If one can arrange it, try and travel between Arundel and Chichester as the sun sets across the Downs. The flat, but peaceful, setting of the route and the numerous pheasants and rabbits in the fields can make for a memorable journey. The line between Ford and Chichester is dead straight, and travelling at speed the train soon arrives at **Barnham**, junction for Bognor Regis. When the wind whips off the sea, Barnham is a raw place to be, and the interior of the small buffet is most welcome. For details of points of interest near Barnham Station see Chapter 9.

The station building at **Bognor Regis** is the third, dating from 1902, and is suitably grandiose for this proud little resort. The suffix 'Regis' was not added until 1929 after King George V's period of residence in the town, but Bognor was fashionable with royalty and the aristocracy in the late eighteenth century. The mixture of sand and shingle beaches, gardens, a large children's zoo, and Butlin's Holiday Camp make Bognor a favourite family resort. Like most of the Sussex coast, Bognor is also favoured by many for retirement. From Bognor Station, the Southdown No. 260 bus runs hourly to Midhurst via Pagham (described in Chapter 9) and Chichester.

Back at Barnham, we change trains to reach Chichester. As we approach the county town of West Sussex, the spire of the cathedral beckons us onward and soon we arrive at **Chichester** (described in Chapter 9). With so many places to visit and things to see along this route, why not take a week exploring the area with a Rail Rover ticket? Who knows, you may even get the author's brother driving the train!

# ARUNDEL
### by Laurel Arnison and H. Trevor Jones

Strategically located where the River Arun pierces the South Downs, this picturesque town has roots dating back to before the Norman Conquest, although most of the buildings now in existence are Victorian. Approaching Arundel from the station, you cross the river at an attractive location, with the old town ahead on the hillside, dominated by the castle. Once over the bridge, turn right for the castle, for pleasant riverside walks, and for the Wildfowl Trust. But keep straight on along a narrow road for the central square with its tasteful architecture — no modern 'could be anywhere' shopfronts here! Follow the road uphill beyond the square for the parish church on the right, and later, the cathedral on the left.

Arundel Castle is the seat of the Duke of Norfolk and Earl of Arundel, Lord Marshal of England. The castle is of Norman origin, and was built on the site of an older Anglo-Saxon structure. It was extensively damaged during the Civil War and was largely rebuilt during the eighteenth and nineteenth centuries, when efforts were made to restore a sense of its medieval past — for example, the Baron's Hall — although parts of the original Norman structure still remain. It contains numerous art treasures and examples of period furniture. The castle is open from April to October — telephone Arundel (0903) 883136 for details.

A walk of about a mile through an avenue of trees takes the visitor to Swanbourne Lake (part of Arundel Park) where amusements include feeding the ever-hungry swans and ducks, and boating on the lake. This is also a good starting-point for a walk across the Downs to Amberley.

Wildfowl of a more exotic kind can be found just across the road at the Wildfowl Trust, which is one of seven centres around the country where visitors can make close contact with many different species. Many of the birds are very tame and will take bread and grain (on sale from the centre) from your hands. The site includes a number of strategically placed hides from which the local bird population, which may include water-rail, snipe, or greenshank, can be observed. Real enthusiasts may even be tempted to 'adopt a Duck'! The centre, which also has an excellent café and souvenir shop, is open all year — telephone Arundel 883355 for details.

The town also has two interesting churches, the Parish Church of St Nicolas and the Catholic Cathedral of Our Lady and St Philip Neri. St Nicolas's Church, by far the older of the two, was rebuilt in 1380 after the Black Death. It contains traces of medieval murals on its walls, and its most unusual feature is the Catholic chapel built for the Fitzalan-Howard family. This fell into disrepair after the Dissolution of the Monasteries, and was damaged during the Civil War, only being restored during the nineteenth century. The cathedral was built in French Gothic style between 1869 and 1873. It began life as a parish church, but became a cathedral in 1965 and contains some modern stained-glass windows.

Arundel is now predominantly a leisure town and contains a wide variety of souvenir shops, pubs, and cafés. The Museum and Heritage Centre (telephone 882726), which tells the story of Arundel and its people, is well worth a visit and there is also the Toy and Military Museum (telephone 882908), housed in a Georgian cottage. The town is liable to become extremely congested with traffic in the summer — so leave your car at home and come by train.

# 9
# BRIGHTON–PORTSMOUTH HARBOUR
by Hugh R. Fowler, Mark Hosking, and H. Trevor Jones

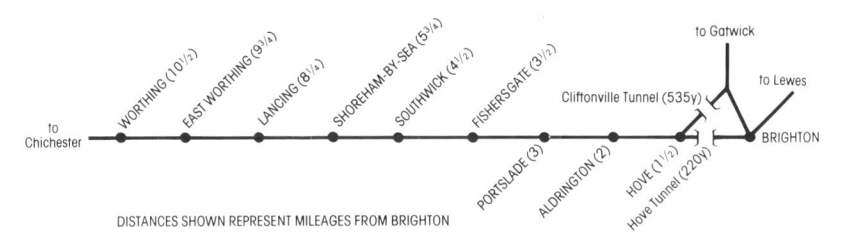

DISTANCES SHOWN REPRESENT MILEAGES FROM BRIGHTON

This line connects two of the most important termini on the South Coast, each having excellent connections with London.

The line to Portsmouth is 46½ miles long, somewhat shorter than the direct road route, and is served by twenty-eight stations, although most trains miss a few of them. Such a concentration of stations is unusual, except in the big conurbations. Thirteen of these are located in the first one-third of the journey, with only three in the next 13 miles to Chichester, and a further twelve in the remainder of the journey.

After leaving **Brighton** (described in Chapter 1), the first stop by nearly every train is at **Hove**, where through trains from London Victoria to Littlehampton and Portsmouth (dividing at Worthing) join the coastal line. Hove does not like to be regarded as part of Brighton, and boasts the headquarters of Sussex County Cricket Club, which in past days has produced some famous English players.

As the train approaches **Southwick**, the fourth station beyond Hove, a power-station to the left is in sight alongside a canal built to give access to the docks. The power-station will soon be closed and the whole dock area redeveloped.

Next comes **Shoreham-by-Sea**, served by most trains. Here is quite a busy little harbour in the estuary of the River Adur (pronounced 'aider'), now mostly filled with pleasure-boats; it is best viewed from a long footbridge across the river, not far from the railway station, for which you turn left out of the station service road into Brunswick Road, where the route will be obvious. On the way you cannot fail to miss the town's main landmark, the Church of St Mary de Haura – considered by some to be among the leading fifty non-cathedral greater churches in the country. This church was built between 1100 and 1225, and is actually just the chancel of a former even larger church. Its unique architectural glory is the two set of bays and arches of the main choir – today's nave: to the north are solid Norman columns supporting highly decorated arches; to the south is a clear first stage of Gothic architecture – the two styles sitting harmoniously together.

Beyond Shoreham Station we see the stump of the old branch to Horsham, now only reaching the cement works near Bramber, a village noted for its ruined Norman castle, destroyed in the Civil War. Also upstream, but only ½ mile away, is Old Shoreham, which was the original village and port until 1100. There was once a Roman settlement here, and the little church contains existing Saxon work at its west end; but there is not much else of interest, unless you are energetic enough to climb the hill another mile to the north (via a minor road or a footpath) for an excellent view over the Adur Valley and the coastal plain westwards.

Almost at once our train crosses the Adur Estuary, with the new road bridge visible on the seaward side, and a good view inland (to the right, from either bridge) up the

41

river to Lancing College, whose imposing chapel on the slope of the Downs rises to 94 feet. Although Lancing has its own station, passengers for the college usually alight at Shoreham. On our right we pass the Brighton, Hove, and Worthing Airport for the use of light aircraft, just across the Adur, before we reach **Lancing** Station, where there is now no trace of the former Southern Railway carriage works.

Next come three stations for **Worthing** (with the principal, formerly Central, in the middle). No longer the holiday resort it once was, Worthing has become the national headquarters of the popular game of bowls. The National Championships are held here each August. Despite having over 90,000 inhabitants, Worthing's main cinema has been demolished, leaving only one with an uncertain future, on a short lease; fortunately, live theatre still flourishes here.

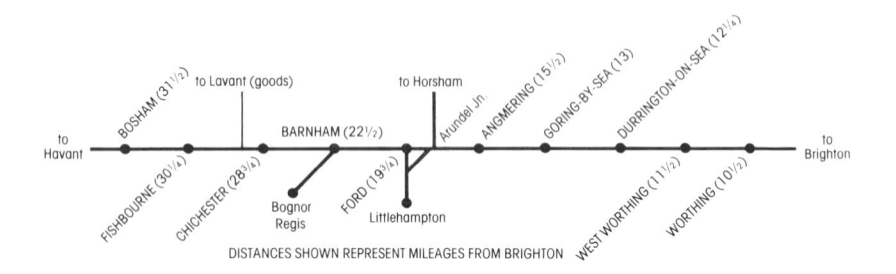

```
to              BOSHAM (31½)   to Lavant (goods)           to Horsham    Arundel Jn.  ANGMERING (15½)  GORING-BY-SEA (13)  DURRINGTON-ON-SEA (12½)            to
Havant                                         BARNHAM (22½)                                                                                                Brighton
         FISHBOURNE (30¼)  CHICHESTER (28¾)         Bognor    FORD (19¾)                                              WEST WORTHING (11½)  WORTHING (10½)
                                                    Regis              Littlehampton
                              DISTANCES SHOWN REPRESENT MILEAGES FROM BRIGHTON
```

The third station – **West Worthing** – is the terminus, stabling, and servicing point for a number of trains. Next comes one of the newer stations, **Durrington-on-Sea**, from which can be seen three large buildings, one of which is a modern sports centre.

**Goring-by-Sea** Station is one of many on this line with level crossings, but a flyover designed many years ago has now been constructed taking through traffic over the line. Goring serves a large residential area, including Ferring which may one day have its own station. Many of the housing estates in this area are on the site of former nurseries and market gardens, of which few remain. Highdown Hill just over a mile to the north-east provides a good local viewpoint.

Next comes **Angmering** Station, which serves not only Angmering village to the north of the line, but also the growing district of Rustington, noted for its free car parking. Although this area suffered much devastation in the October 1987 hurricane, there is now little sign of the damage it caused.

Approaching the River Arun, there are two junctions close together: at the first the line from Horsham and Arundel comes in on the right and the branch to Littlehampton (see Chapter 8) goes off to the left; then at the second, immediately before the Arun is crossed, a line comes in from Littlehampton, completing a triangle on the left. To the right we get a fine view both of Arundel Castle, seat of the Duke of Norfolk, and of the lofty Roman Catholic Cathedral built in 1870. This is one of the most beautiful tracts of country, if not the most beautiful, on the whole route. For details of Arundel see Chapter 8.

The modern village of **Barnham**, mostly running north-west from the junction station, need not detain the visitor. But turn right out of the station, pass under the railway bridge, and then turn right again down a little lane to reach the ancient settlement nearly a mile away. Here lies Barnham Court, a beautiful old Dutch gabled house of brick. Next to it, is the lovely little Church of St Mary, recorded in 'Domesday Book' in 1086, and almost certainly dating back to Saxon times. The Bellcote, a sort of miniature bell-tower surmounting the west end is one of the few remaining 'White Caps', as these are known in Sussex. Its bell, cast in 1348, is one of the oldest in Sussex. The south wall of the nave is the oldest part of the existing building, dating from about 1100, and includes two characteristic Early Norman windows.

From Barnham there is a branch to Bognor Regis (described in Chapter 8), mostly taken by trains from London via Gatwick and Horsham and also by local trains starting either at Barnham itself or at Littlehampton; Coastway trains tend to keep straight on for Chichester and Portsmouth – at least in the 1987–88 timetable.

The coastline becomes much more interesting west of Bognor Regis where it merges into the village of Pagham, on the shore of Pagham Harbour. This is one of the few remaining undeveloped parts of the Sussex coast – indeed the Cuckmere Estuary and Seven Sisters (see Chapter 5) is the only other. Pagham Harbour is a natural harbour, but is now only suitable for small pleasure-boats, for it comprises a large and relatively undisturbed area of tidal mudflats and saltings, intersected by numerous channels. Since 1965 the area has been a Local Nature Reserve managed by West Sussex County Council. But in the thirteenth century Pagham was the ninth largest port and the fourth wealthiest parish in England. Its parish church is dedicated to St Thomas à Becket who was murdered in Canterbury Cathedral in 1170; the present church was probably built within forty years of his death. But Christian worship at Pagham goes back to the seventh century, the remains of not only an earlier Norman church but also a smaller Saxon stone church having been found on the present site. There is an hourly bus (Southdown No. 260) from Midhurst to Bognor railway station via Chichester bus station and Pagham beach.

Pagham Harbour is, however, best reached by the Selsey bus (Southdown Nos 250 and 251) from Chichester bus station (opposite the railway station), because the Information Centre and best access point is actually on the B2145 along which the bus passes, every half hour each way. If coming at lunchtime, you are recommended to alight in the village of Sidlesham and walk down a side road to the left to the head of a little creek, where a tasty bar snack can be obtained in the local pub just round the corner. There are footpaths all along both the north and south sides of the harbour. The first section on the north side is covered at most high tides, but it can be bypassed by taking the little lane inland and then an alternative path across a field. It is a popular area for bird-spotting, particularly on the southern shingle bank that almost cuts the harbour off from the sea. Its prime importance is as a wintering area for wildfowl and waders and as an important breeding-ground. Little terns and ringed plovers are of special interest, and there is also considerable botanical interest.

South-west of Pagham Harbour is Selsey Bill (Bill means 'point'), complete with holiday camp, notwithstanding the largely shingle beach. The area around the point is low and largely built-up, but there are, on a clear day, good views of the Isle of Wight from the west side. It is possible to walk along the front from Pagham Harbour until just short of the point (which is privately owned), as long as you do not mind walking on shingle. Notice the fast currents swirling around the headland, and look out for the stalls selling locally caught shellfish.

From Barnham the main Coastway line heads straight for the city of Chichester across the top of Selsey Bill. To the north the Downs stand sentinel over the low-lying coastal ground, their rolling crowns allowing the railway passenger occasional glimpses of local landmarks such as Halnaker Windmill and the grandstand at Goodwood Racecourse.

As the line approaches **Chichester**, it passes on the right a network of man-made lakes, known locally as 'The Pits'. These were created some decades ago for the extraction and processing of gravel, but most have now ceased working. However, with the recent boom in the leisure industry, many have adapted their calm, shallow waters to provide facilities for a variety of water-sports, from sailboarding to water-

Chichester

skiing. The site visible from the train still performs its original function and serves as a terminal to receive, wash, and store gravel extracted from clay workings a few miles to the north-west of the city; the transfer is performed by a train of privately owned wagons. For a description of Chichester see below.

The railway sweeps out of Chichester on a long smooth curve, with limited views of the cathedral. As the curve changes more sharply to bring the line back on to its westerly course, the old Midhurst branch cuts off to the north, now only used for 2 miles as far as Lavant by the gravel train.

As it approaches **Fishbourne** the line passes close to the Roman villa, recognisable as a long low building on the left-hand side. This is one of Britain's largest excavated Roman sites, presenting what archaeologists believe to be an accurate picture of local life in the first century AD. The pride of the site are the exquisitely restored mosaic floors presented along with models, artefacts, and even a garden laid out in its original position and style. To reach the villa, once the home of the area's Roman Governor, turn right out of the station and then turn left into Roman Way. The site is open all year (telephone Chichester 785859).

The line continues to **Bosham** Station (situated in the modern village of Broadridge), where the present down-side buildings, positively oozing country-station charm, were built about the turn of the century. The village of Bosham itself lies a mile to the south, but the walk is worth it, even in the worst weather. The village is situated at the head of one of the creeks inland off Chichester Harbour. To reach it from Bosham Station, turn left out of the station into the B2146, which has a level crossing over the railway; keep straight on across the main A27 coast road; then turn right at a T-junction in order to reach the old centre of Bosham on a low promontory into the creek – the Bosham Channel. Reputedly the site of King Canute's attempt to turn the tide, this pretty harbourside village exudes legend and fairy-tale.

Bosham was an important Roman landing-place, being a sheltered spot where the local tribes were friendly to the Romans – hence the Roman villa at nearby Fishbourne. Bosham also remained important in Saxon times, being the oldest site of Christianity in Sussex. Whether or not King Canute commanded the waves to retire here, his daugher who died in 1035 is almost certainly buried in the church — an eight-year-old child's coffin of the period was uncovered in 1865. The present church is certainly Saxon (early eleventh century) and was probably rebuilt by Canute on the site of an earlier church, itself situated on the site of a Roman basilica.

Built as much in the water as around it, many a village parlour has suffered from a particularly vicious spring tide, and in the summer the locals watch with restrained amusement as the uninformed visitor tries to rescue his car from the merciless grip of the tide. Earthworks surrounding the harbour to protect the low-lying pastures from the sea have been known to the locals as 'chairs' for centuries, and the local version of the legend has it that the first of these sea defences was constructed by Canute to protect his own local residence. Today Bosham is a quiet little village, mostly frequented by yachtsmen. The street along its southern shore is liable to flooding at high tide.

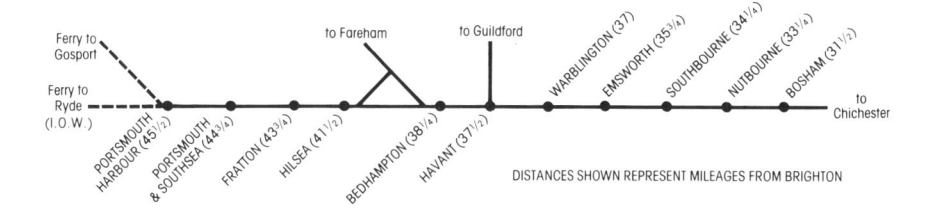

DISTANCES SHOWN REPRESENT MILEAGES FROM BRIGHTON

From Bosham the line rises above the nearby natural harbours, and heads for the sprawling urban mass that has grown up around the top of Portsea Island. **Nutbourne** and **Southbourne** are both villages that have used their halts, constructed in 1906 at the same time as Fishbourne, to encourage housing developments, providing nearly rural homes for many Portsmouth workers.

Crossing from West Sussex into Hampshire the line arrives at **Emsworth**, a small town built around another arm of the harbour network. The town once possessed a number of mills, giving its water frontage a vaguely industrial air, although here, too, pleasure craft now dominate. The town centre remains virtually unspoilt, with small shops abounding, now either yacht chandlers or antique dealers, and a couple of suitably nautical hostelries.

On from Emsworth the line passes **Warblington**, another 'Motor Train' halt built to serve the eastern edge of Havant, and reaches the junction with the mainline from Waterloo. From this point on, through **Havant** Station just a few hundred yards distant, and on into Portsmouth itself, the line was at one time operated jointly by the LBSCR and the LSWR. The remainder of the journey into Portsmouth is described in Chapter 12.

On the west side of Chichester Harbour is Hayling Island, which can be reached by bus from Havant Station, passing over a bridge to the island. The south-east and south-west corners of Hayling Island have interesting coastal features but the central beach area is more geared to the amusement-arcade fraternity. It can, however, be quite exhilarating to stand on the front or shelter in a pub at a high spring tide when a strong south-westerly wind causes great waves to splash over the promenade or against the pub windows with tremendous force. There is no ferry to West Wittering, but at the west end of Hayling Island there is a passenger ferry approximately every hour to Portsmouth. However, the buses each side of the ferry are summer only; in winter you have quite a walk at each end to and from the nearest bus.

# CHICHESTER

### by Mark Hosking and Laurel Arnison

Chichester, the county town of West Sussex, has a history dating back to at least Roman times, when it was known as 'Noviomagus'. The Romans were followed by the Saxons, who used the word 'Caester' to describe all Roman towns. Aella, King of the West Saxons, is reputed to have offered Noviomagus to his son Cissa. Thus it became known as 'Cissa's Caester' and, eventually, Chichester. Chichester has been continually occupied ever since, and both the town and the surrounding area boast an impressive array of historical sites that reflect the rich history of this corner of Sussex.

**Chichester** Station is situated only a five-minute stroll from the town centre. This stroll, northwards along South Street having turned left out of the station service road, introduces the visitor to some of the delights of this ancient market town. Not a building stands more than four storeys high, and most new developments have tried, if not always with success, to blend in with the established character of the city.

Through traffic is kept to a ring road away from the centre, and much of the area around the medieval market cross, at the crossroads of the town's four main streets, has been pedestrianised, allowing the visitor to stand and look without being disturbed by throbbing traffic. This cross was built at the end of the fifteenth century and has been described as the finest structure of its kind in the country.

About two-thirds of the way up South Street from the station, on the left, is a narrow lane called 'Canon Lane', easily recognisable by the gatehouse standing above it. This leads into the cathedral precincts, with their fine Georgian and Victorian houses for the clergy, and cottage-lined alleyways. Continuing along Canon Lane beneath another gatehouse brings the visitor into the Bishop's Palace Gardens. To the right a gravel drive sweeps up to the palace itself, while to the left discreet signposts indicate the path through the public part of the gardens. These afford excellent views of the cathedral's west face, while the high garden wall is part of the city's original Roman fortifications.

The network of paths converge on another gate with exits on to the ring road. Turning right and then right again leads into West Street and back to the city centre past the cathedral itself, immediately notable for its detached bell-tower. Chichester Cathedral was originally founded by St Wilfrid in AD 861, but was moved by the Normans as the sea advanced about 900 years ago. Worthy of note are the unusual Arundel Screen separating the nave from the chancel, the bold and vivid tapestry hung behind the altar with its symbolic representations of the Apostles, and the Shrine of St Richard of Chichester, a place of great importance to the medieval pilgrim. Also inside the cathedral are, *inter alia,* two twelfth-century sculptures, a controversial painting by Graham Sutherland, Marc Chagall's stained-glass window based on Psalm 150, and the superb 1983 font made from Cornish stone and copper.

At the far north end of North Street, across Oaklands Park is Chichester's world-famous Festival Theatre. Opened in 1962 under the personal guidance of Sir Lawrence Olivier, the theatre's annual season now provides a broad spectrum across the arts, from rock to opera, and Shakespeare to modernist drama. Many prospective London shows rise or fall on their reception in Chichester's delightful setting.

Return towards the station via Priory Park, reached by turning left off North Street at the Ship Hotel. The mound at the top of the park was once the city's castle, whose chapel, still standing, is now used as a museum; and Sussex County cricket was once played in the shadow of the trees lining the castle wall.

Back streets take the visitor on to East Street, across which are the Georgian streets known as 'The Pallants'. These four streets meet at a crossroads on one corner of which is Pallant House, whose doorway is guarded by a pair of stone Dodo birds! Pallant

House dates from 1712 and is one of the finest Queen Anne houses in the country – it is at present undergoing restoration to its original eighteenth-century style.

The history of the town is continued in the District Museum in Little London, open all the year from Tuesday to Saturday, admission free (telephone 784683). The town has many fine restaurants, cafés, and pubs to relax in, a good array of fashionable shops, and a beautifully designed modern theatre – just the thing to round off an enjoyable day in this haven of Sussex culture.

Chichester bus station lies opposite the railway station. Three services may be of interest: the No. 260 which travels through the Downs to Midhurst; Nos 250 and 251 which go past Pagham Harbour Nature Reserve to Selsey, as described above; and the half-hourly Nos 252 and 253 to East and West Wittering (with their many sandy beaches), which pass within walking distance of several villages such as Itchenor and Birdham on the south-east banks of Chichester Harbour.

A short trip on the Southdown No. 260 bus travelling in the Midhurst direction, takes the visitor to Singleton, home of the Weald and Downland Open Air Museum and West Dean Gardens. The museum contains reconstructed houses and cottages dating back to the thirteenth century, all of which are open to the public. The museum is open all year – for details telephone Singleton (024363) 348. West Dean Gardens were originally the grounds of an Edwardian country house but are now part of an art and craft college. Their 35 acres allow peaceful walks and the opportunity to look for rare botanical specimens. The gardens are open daily from 1 April to 30 September, from 11 a.m. to 6 p.m. (telephone Singleton 301). You can also walk up the hill to the south-east of West Dean village to The Trundle, an ancient hilltop fort which affords excellent views across the Goodwood estate towards Chichester and its harbours to the south, and to Goodwood Racecourse, set amid rolling downland to the north.

# 10
## GUILDFORD–REDHILL
### by I. McGill

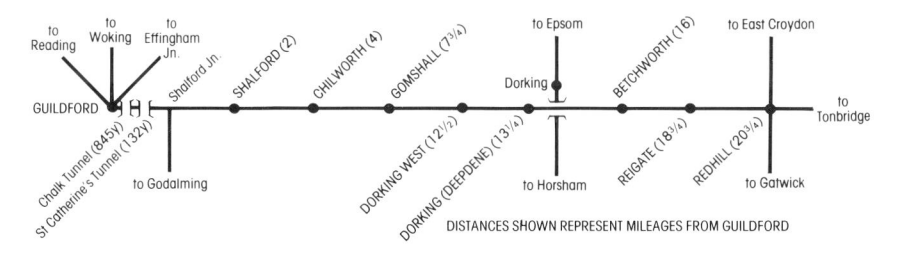

DISTANCES SHOWN REPRESENT MILEAGES FROM GUILDFORD

The first railway to reach Guildford arrived in 1845, and four years later the line from Redhill was completed. This connected with the existing SER line from London to Dover via Redhill (see Chapter 1). The SER was thus able to reach, by means of a long, straggling cross-country route, a far-flung outpost at Reading.

**Guildford** is a busy junction, at the focal point of five rail routes, and is served by both diesel and electric trains. The journey to **Redhill** is by DMU, and takes just over thirty minutes by the hourly Reading–Gatwick trains, which call at **Dorking (Deepdene)** and **Reigate** *en route*. **Gomshall** is served about every two hours, with additional trains at weekday peak times, which also call at the remaining intermediate stations. Otherwise, the service at **Shalford**, **Chilworth**, and

Gomshall.

**Betchworth** is sparse and irregular with no trains on Sundays. Nevertheless, with some judicious planning, perhaps in conjunction with bus services along the adjacent A25, these stations can usefully form part of an itinerary for some rewarding excursions. All intermediate stations, except **Reigate**, are unstaffed, but tickets can be purchased on the train.

Leaving **Guildford**, the train plunges into the 845-yard-long Chalk Tunnel, followed quite quickly by the shorter St Catherine's Tunnel, to emerge into open country for the brief run to Shalford Junction. Here we part company with the mainline to Portsmouth (described in Chapter 12), and swing eastwards on to non-electrified metals, crossing the Wey Navigation by an impressive girder bridge. The River Wey was canalised for much of its length in the seventeenth century, and became an important commercial artery between Godalming and the Thames at Weybridge, but nowadays it is used mainly by pleasure craft.

At this point, a tree-clad embankment comes in from the right, to end abruptly at the water's edge. These abandoned earthworks are the remains of a spur which was intended to allow trains from Portsmouth to reach London via Redhill. Passing beneath the A281, the train then runs into the station at **Shalford** where the platforms, devoid of all but minimal shelter, are linked by footbridge.

The nucleus of the village is in the vicinity of the station and around the grassy expanse of Shalford Common, but ribbon development extends northwards so that it is now virtually coterminous with Guildford. Shalford Mill is powered by the waters of the Tillingbourne, and dates from the eighteenth century. Now in the care of the National Trust, it is open daily and is within walking distance of the station and bus stops, just off the main road, here called 'The Street'.

The railway follows the valley of the diminutive Tillingbourne to reach **Chilworth**, where the main buildings still survive, close by the level crossing at the Guildford end of the platforms. Chilworth shelters beneath the ridge where the Chapel of St Martha lies hidden and lonely in sylvan seclusion. This historic local landmark may be reached via Blacksmith Lane, thence by bridleway and footpath, whence the walk can be continued over Pewley Down towards Guildford, or extended along the Pilgrims' Way, which follows the ridge eastwards over Netley Heath and Ranmore Common, towards Dorking.

Gunpowder was manufactured at Chilworth from the seventeenth century until 1920, and the works were once connected to the station by a tramway. Traces of this, and remains of the powder-mills, can still be found along the Tillingbourne. The gardens of nearby Albury Park, and the reception rooms of the Victorian mansion are open to visitors (telephone 0486 412964 for details).

Beyond Chilworth, the railway parts company with the river, swinging south in a wide arc to avoid Albury Park, and a switchback of taxing gradients — which is best appreciated from a seat with a forward or rear view through the driver's cab — begins in earnest. There is an exhilarating descent to reach **Gomshall** (pronounced 'gum-shall') Station, which is well sited in the village and is also convenient for the neighbouring villages of Shere and Abinger Hammer. This lovely area is marred only by the heavy traffic on the A25.

Gomshall water-mill now houses a shop and restaurant, but the water-wheel and some machinery remain, and the premises are open daily except on Mondays. There has been a tanning industry at Gomshall for centuries, while nearby Abinger Hammer developed as a centre of the ancient Wealden iron industry. The second element of the village name is derived from the water-powered hammers of the long-defunct forge. Today the waters of the Tillingbourne flow unharnessed, and the extensive local watercress-beds are sustained by fresh water from deep boreholes. The outstanding feature of the village, which has appeared on countless calendars and greetings cards, is undoubtedly the unique clock projecting above the road, and its figure of a smith who strikes the hours with a hammer.

Less than a mile away lies Shere, which has been claimed by some to be the prettiest village in Surrey. Its timber-framed and other buildings preserve something of the character of former years. Lower Street provides a pleasant stroll near the river, or in the other direction the village square leads to the church entrance.

As a railhead for the walker and cyclist, Gomshall is well placed and, with a good map as your guide, offers many attractive possibilities. Quiet lanes and byways lead south to the wooded country of the Greensand Ridge and remote unspoilt villages like Friday Street, Abinger, Holmbury St Mary, and Sutton. Tracks lead invitingly on to the North Downs, whence one may strike out across Netley Heath towards the Silent Pool, so called because the surface of its clear waters is scarcely sullied by a ripple from the streams by which it is fed. Paths continue towards the 567-feet summit at Newlands Corner, from where you can enjoy one of the finest panoramas in south-east England.

Beyond Gomshall, the railway sweeps round the southern flank of the Downs for some 5 miles towards Dorking, the heavily wooded Greensand Ridge prominent on the right, rising in sylvan splendour to attain a summit of 965 feet at Leith Hill, about 4 miles distant, and the highest point east of the Mendips. The top of the tower which crowns its summit is 1,000 feet above sea-level, and the view is reputed to range over a dozen counties.

Nearby Leith Hill Place dates from the seventeenth century and was once owned by the Wedgwood family. The property subsequently passed to the Vaughan Williams family, and was left to the National Trust by Dr Ralph Vaughan Williams, the composer. Unfortunately neither the house nor gardens are normally open to the public. To the left, the chalk downs climb steeply from the line with, perhaps, a glimpse of the spire of Ranmore Church high above the trees. Away to the right Westcott, home of the seventeenth-century diarist John Evelyn, may be seen across the fields, with the slender spire of Dorking Parish Church beyond, as the train nears **Dorking West** (formerly **Dorking Town**) Station.

The open platforms here are provided with bus-stop-type shelters and connected by subway. The town is reached by walking down Station Road and turning left into West Street. The steep ascent to Ranmore Common can be made by turning sharp left at the end of the station approach and left again into Ranmore Road, a distance of about a mile. In a further two or three minutes, the train passes over a bridge spanning the busy London Road, to arrive at **Dorking (Deepdene)** Station where, because of its better service, most visitors are likely to arrive.

The station owes its name to Deepdene House, a fine mansion which once stood about a mile away. Although less convenient for the town than **Dorking West**, **Deepdene** is close to **Dorking** Station with its regular service of electric trains to London (described in Chapter 7) and walkers bound for Ranmore Common may find it a useful starting-point. There are buses to the town centre, but do not rely on one unless you know the times.

Whatever your goal, descend the steps to street-level, and turn right. In a few moments you will see the modern façade of Dorking Station at the end of its approach road on your right, where there are bus stops and a taxi rank. Directions to the town centre are given in Chapter 7.

An attractive country town on the route of the old Roman Stane Street, which ran from London to Chichester, Dorking has given its name to an ancient breed of poultry which is thought to have been developed by the Romans. Markets have been held since Edward I granted the town its Charter in the twelfth century, and among the more interesting buildings is the partly timbered White Horse in the High Street, which continues to offer hospitality to visitors.

Buses to the surrounding districts stop near by, but some are few and far between. However London Country South-West operates a very useful Ramblers Bus No. 417 which serves Dorking and Gomshall stations (for details see Chapter 7).

Box Hill comes into view as the train leaves **Deepdene** and crosses above the electrified line from Leatherhead to Horsham (see Chapter 7). Dorking Station is below to the left, but little trace remains of a spur which once linked the two lines. Castle Mill with its water-wheel can be seen across the meadows to the right, and then there are glimpses of the villages at Brockham and Betchworth as the train continues in the shadow of Box Hill — whose tree-less southern slopes are in marked contrast to the wooded escarpment west of Dorking.

A huge white scar on the hillside to the left marks the site of the former Greystone Lime Company's Betchworth Quarry. The works were served by extensive internal railways of 3 foot 2¼ inch and 1 foot 6 inch gauge as well as the network of standard-gauge sidings. A narrow-gauge museum was set up on this site, but in 1982 the exhibits were moved to the Chalk Pits Museum at Amberley in Sussex (described in Chapter 8).

**Betchworth** Station narrowly escaped closure in 1954, and survives today in basic form as two empty platforms almost bereft of fittings, except for the nicely restored gas-lamps. The station house still stands by the level crossing at the Redhill end of the platforms. Betchworth village is about a mile to the south, its lovely cottages standing on the banks of the River Mole.

The North Downs gradually recede, and there follows a long straight run across the meadows towards Reigate. Soon farmland gives way to an urban landscape, **Reigate** Station is approached over a busy level crossing and conductor rails are once again in evidence, the short stretch of line from Redhill having been electrified in 1932.

Nowadays electric trains only appear at Reigate during the rush hours; at other periods the basic hourly service of diesel trains is supplemented by some short workings to and from Redhill provided by Tonbridge line DMUs. Reigate retains its station buildings, and the signal-box which controls the busy level crossing. The platforms here are connected by a subway, and there is a stabling siding for electric trains.

Reigate is an ancient market town which has managed to retain a good deal of character, and some interesting buildings. These include the old Town Hall of 1728 in the High Street, the eighteenth-century Reigate Priory in Bell Street, and a sixteenth-century cottage in quaintly named Slipshoe Street. Little, however, remains of the castle, except some earthworks atop a mound behind the High Street.

Reigate can also boast two windmills: a fine brick tower-mill on Wray Common and a post-mill on the open expanse of Reigate Heath, which lies to the south-west of the town. The latter, which stands at the site once occupied by a gallows, is the more interesting. The base was converted to a place of worship in 1880, and services are still held at 3 p.m. on the third Sunday of every month from May to October. Visitors are admitted at other times, and the key can be obtained from the adjacent golf club house if the premises are locked.

After leaving Reigate Station, the train wends its way through the area where Reigate becomes one with its neighbour Redhill. After rounding a curve to cross high above the Brighton Road, it joins the main London to Brighton line to run alongside one of the two faces of the island platform at Redhill.

# 11

## LONDON WATERLOO–GUILDFORD VIA COBHAM

### by I. McGill

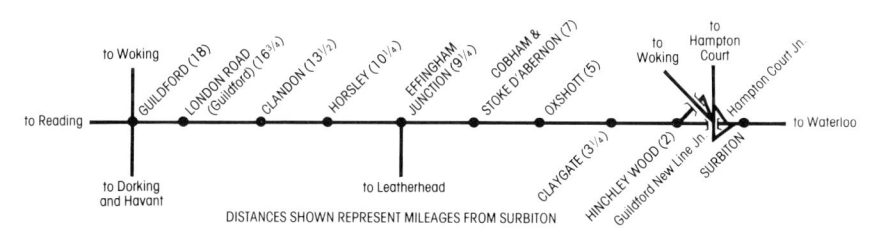

The Guildford New Line ('New' because it was opened in 1885, after the original route through Woking) leaves the mainline just beyond Surbiton, to make its way across country in a south-westerly direction. Electrification reached Claygate as early as 1916, and was extended to Guildford in 1925. There is a regular half-hourly train service (hourly on Sundays), which is augmented at peak times.

From Waterloo to Surbiton we follow the mainline to Portsmouth and Bournemouth (described in Chapter 12). The present **Surbiton** Station is the result of rebuilding during 1937–38 by the Southern Railway in its distinctive style – typical of the company's architecture and totally in keeping with the brave, dynamic new world of Southern Electric.

After passing Long Ditton, the train enters Surrey, and soon reaches Hampton Court Junction. At this point the mainline divests itself of both the Hampton Court branch and the new line to Guildford, which curves away to the left past spacious gardens. The up and down lines diverge independently, to be reunited at the apex of a triangle in which is situated **Hinchley Wood** Station, opened in 1930 to serve an expanding residential area.

Probing tongues of greenery are an increasing feature of the scene until, beyond Claygate, town gives way to country. However, the transition is somewhat illusory, for soon a line of pylons stalk menacingly across our way, and then the meadows are rent by the Esher bypass. Away to the left, the woodland over towards Chessington merges into Princes Covert, while opposite, Esher Common is lost to view as the pines of Oxshott Heath close in.

**Claygate** and **Oxshott** stations are both within reach of the magnificently restored Claremont Gardens, which became National Trust property in 1949. Begun before 1720, it is the earliest surviving example of the English landscape garden. The present house, which is not Trust property, was built for Clive of India, and dates from 1772. Oxshott Station probably offers the best approach, by way of the heath and Black Pond, to gain the A3 Portsmouth Road (a good up-to-date street atlas or two-and-a-half-inch Ordnance Survey map is recommended).

The cool, pine-scented glades of Oxshott Heath persist for some distance until, emerging from a cutting, the line is bordered by the smooth green acres of Knott Park, before we arrive at **Cobham and Stoke D'Abernon**. In common with many other suburban stations, the former goods yard has become a car park. If you are travelling on a weekday it is likely to be filled, as are those at neighbouring stations, with parked vehicles – waiting like obedient dogs for their masters to return from Town.

Stoke D'Abernon consists of little more than a church and manor house, reached within a few minutes' walk from the station by turning right into Stoke Road. Standing serenely beside the river, the Church of St Mary is renowned for possessing the oldest memorial brass in England, dating from 1277. Across Stoke D'Abernon Bridge is the Yehudi Menuhin Music School, and a fine Jacobean house called 'Slyfield'.

Cobham is in the opposite direction and consists, strictly speaking, of Street Cobham on the Portsmouth Road, and Church Cobham, rather closer to the station. Nowadays, however, the distinction is somewhat academic, as indiscriminate building has compelled them to merge. In the seventeenth century a group of agricultural workers calling themselves 'Diggers' tried to set up a kind of commune, but were routed by the squire and the vicar, on the pretext that the group were anarchists. Cedar House, which dates from the eighteenth century, is in the care of the National Trust, but only accessible by prior arrangement. One of its outstanding features is the open-timbered roof of its great hall.

By way of contrast, a totally different, but no less interesting building can be found near the A3 on Chatley Heath, should you have the time and energy to undertake

A train approaches Effingham Junction, where the line from Leatherhead meets the Guildford New Line (Photo: John C. Baker)

the walk. There you will find a five-storey tower, once part of a chain of semaphore stations which were completed in 1822. They were erected at 5- and 10-mile intervals to facilitate the exchange of signals between the Admiralty in London, and Portsmouth Dockyard. So efficient was the system that a message could be sent in under a minute!

Crossing the River Mole, which once powered Cobham Mill, Downside Farm can be seen on the right, with Downside village beyond, while on the opposite side Muggeridge Wood disperses to reveal the M25 scything its way relentlessly across the landscape. Rural calm is swiftly restored, with views towards Bookham Common, before the train passes Newmarsh Farm to be engulfed by woodland from which the Leatherhead line emerges at **Effingham Junction**.

Anyone not familiar with the area may be forgiven for not having heard of this station, but along the road the Lord Howard public house is a reminder that it was Lord Howard of Effingham who led the English fleet to victory against the Spanish Armada in 1588. Effingham village is nearly 2 miles to the south, across Effingham Common. London Country operates an infrequent bus service, but on a fine day a series of footpaths and bridleways, some of which also lead towards Bookham and East Horsley, offer a pleasant alternative.

Drawing clear of Effingham Junction, the large carriage sheds on the left come as a surprise amid isolated and sylvan surroundings, with Barnsthorns Wood closing in as we begin the short run to **Horsley**. This station is roughly midway between Ockham to the north, with its water-mill, and East Horsley on the A246 to the south. Horsley Tower is a mock-Elizabethan mansion, contemporary with East Horsley, which was rebuilt largely with flint as a 'model' village early last century. South of the village, tracks lead tantalisingly over Netley Heath to Guildford, Gomshall, and Ranmore.

West Horsley is glimpsed on the left as the train continues on its way past Gason Wood, with distant views of Netley Heath above the trees. **Clandon** Station is actually in West Clandon, a village strung out along the road bordering Clandon Park, which is the setting for Clandon House, a Palladian-style country house cared for by the National Trust.

Built for the second Lord Onslow, the house contains a famous collection of needlework, furniture, and porcelain, as well as the Museum of the Queen's Royal Surrey Regiment. The entrance is about ¾ mile south of the station, along the A247. Clandon Park is not a Trust property and is, therefore, not open to the public.

Bridleways and footpaths in the vicinity lead over the Downs to Newlands Corner and the Silent Pool (see Chapter 10). The National Trust is also custodian of Hatchlands, a mansion built for Admiral Boscawen, who defeated the French fleet at Louisburg in 1758. This neighbouring property lies beyond East Clandon on the A246 towards Horsley, and is rather more than 2 miles towards Clandon, the nearest station.

Guildford is now only a few miles away, and soon the fields and woodland on either side yield to a more urban environment as the train runs through the outlying districts of Merrow and Abbotswood.

**London Road** Station serves a predominantly residential area, and takes its name from the thoroughfare which crosses above the line adjacent to the platforms. It is a less strenuous walk to most of central Guildford from here than from the main station. To reach the town centre from London Road Station, turn left out of the main exit and proceed to the traffic lights, then turn right into London Road and continue straight ahead.

There is a commanding view across town as the railway is carried high above the rooftops and over the River Wey. Our train curves round in an arc to the south, past the panel signal-box and comes to a stand alongside Platform 1 at **Guildford** Station.

A footbridge and subway give access to the other platforms; the footbridge also has an exit (not always open) which is convenient for the cathedral and university. The main exit is ahead on your left.

# LEATHERHEAD–EFFINGHAM JUNCTION
## by I. McGill

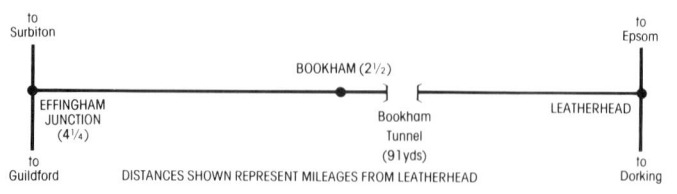

```
to                                                                    to
Surbiton                                                              Epsom
   |                                                                    |
   |                        BOOKHAM (2½)                                |
   |                              |                                     |
   ●————————————————————————————●—————————————————————————————————●
   EFFINGHAM                  Bookham                          LEATHERHEAD
   JUNCTION                   Tunnel
   (4¼)                       (91yds)
   to
   Guildford     DISTANCES SHOWN REPRESENT MILEAGES FROM LEATHERHEAD    to
                                                                      Dorking
```

This short stretch of line has an hourly off-peak train service throughout the week including Sundays, which provides connections at Effingham with the Waterloo–Guildford via Cobham service (described above). The line, which was electrified in 1925, is served by EMUs which work to and from Waterloo via Epsom.

After leaving the Dorking line behind at **Leatherhead**, trains for Effingham curve sharply to the right to cross the River Mole and pass close to Canons Court. Box Hill and the North Downs provide a verdant backdrop to the houses of Fetcham which nudge the lineside on the left. Meanwhile, the fields sloping down to the river opposite give way to an area of glasshouses, and the railway plunges into a long, well-timbered cutting, which culminates in the short Bookham Tunnel.

**Bookham** Station is wedged between the northward sprawl of mostly modern development and the extensive tracts of Bookham and Banks commons. A gate on the up platform gives direct access to the commons, which are criss-crossed by paths and bridleways leading north towards Stoke D'Abernon and westwards to Effingham Junction.

Despite the threat of being swamped by commuterland the Bookhams, which lie south of the station, still retain a good deal of character, and possess an unusual village hall which dates from the fifteenth century, having started life as a tithe barn. Great Bookham Church contains some fine monuments, including fragments of eleventh-century frescos, while that at Little Bookham has a Norman font. Jane Austen often visited Bookham, and may have used it as the basis for Hartfield in her novel *Emma*. Fanny Burney once lived at Fairfield House in the High Street, before moving to Camilla Lacey, near Box Hill. Beyond the A246 tracks lead onwards to Polesden Lacey and Ranmore (see Chapter 10).

After **Bookham** Station there is a shallow cutting, from which the line emerges into dense woodland. Norwood Farm may be seen through the trees on the left as the train rounds a curve at Bushy Thicket, where it joins the line from Surbiton at **Effingham Junction**. Hidden near by in Great Lee Wood are the remains of a moated manor, and at Norwood Farm, which you may have seen from the train, there is a seventeenth-century tithe barn.

# A WALK ROUND GUILDFORD
## by Clive Davies, John Barfield, and I. McGill

Guildford, the county town of Surrey, grew up on a hillside overlooking an important crossing of the River Wey, where it cuts through the North Downs. Prehistoric tracks descending from the chalk ridge followed a route later taken by the London to Portsmouth road, and corresponding with Guildford's present steep High Street, to cross the river. Another ancient route, the Pilgrims' Way, runs along the south side of the hills; it was popularly supposed to have been the path taken by the devout on their way from Winchester to Canterbury.

The town has both a cathedral and a university, each recent acquisitions. The latter is a modern foundation whose yellow-brick buildings colonise the northern slopes of Stag Hill, and although not visible from the town centre, may be seen to advantage from Reading and Ascot line trains as they curve round the foot of the hill. Centre of the Diocese of Guildford, which was created in 1927, the Cathedral of the Holy Spirit is a modern interpretation of the traditional Gothic style, using local red brick. Crowning the summit of Stag Hill, it is clearly visible from much of the town and surrounding countryside. Proposals to build a new County Hall at Stoke Park to the north-east of the centre would have consolidated the town's status, but failed to gain acceptance and were abandoned about ten years ago. As a result, Surrey is unique in being the only county whose administrative headquarters lie outside its own boundaries – at Kingston upon Thames – which is also the centre of a London borough.

Today Guildford is a major shopping centre, serving West Surrey and parts of Hampshire. It has two department stores, several indoor shopping arcades, and a street market. The centre consists of two parallel main streets – North Street, where the street market is held every Friday and Saturday; and High Street, well known for the Guildhall and its clock which overhangs the cobbled street.

Guildford Station is located beyond the left bank of the River Wey on the western edge of the town centre. To get to the main shopping centre and the High Street, you will need to cross the ring road by means of the subways and walkways.

Our description of the town assumes that we are walking up the High Street from the Town Bridge. Most visitors will inevitably be drawn across Onslow Bridge away from the maze of roads to the right. Turn left at the end of the station approach road (car park exit) and cross the river. At the T-junction at the end of the road, go over the pedestrian crossing and turn right. Continue until you reach the bottom of North Street on your left. To get to the High Street, continue in the same direction, going past the Tesco store and along the pedestrianised Friary Street.

To get to the bus station, follow the road as it bears left in a semicircle first into North Street and then into the Friary Shopping Centre. The principal bus operators at the time of writing are Alder Valley and London Country South-West; there are also a number of useful rural services which are operated by the Tillingbourne Bus Company.

The Wey & Godalming Navigations, now owned by the National Trust, rendered the River Wey navigable by means of locks and weirs, being opened as far as Guildford in 1653 and to Godalming in 1733. The waterway became a vital commercial link, but is now only used by pleasure craft, the carriage of goods having succumbed to competition from rail and road haulage. On the right over the bridge next to the Old People's Centre, there is a restored treadmill crane, once worked by convicts.

Returning over the bridge, to the right beyond Debenhams store, and almost on an island site, is the Yvonne Arnaud Theatre, near which is an old water-mill, at present used as a scenery store, but soon to become a second and more intimate theatre. Beyond the Yvonne Arnaud to the left, is Guildford Lock, where people tend to gather to watch the boats pass. On a fine day, one may take a pleasant walk along the towpath, past the weirs, to Guildford Boat House, where boat trips can be booked and craft hired. For a longer walk of about a mile you can continue to St Catherine's Hill with its ruined chapel beside the Pilgrims' Way, by leaving the towpath at an unmarked turning on the right, near a point where sand has been eroded from the hillside. The effort will be rewarded by fine views of the Wey Valley.

Retracing your steps past the old mill, cross the road and climb up the narrow

Rosemary Alley which leads to Quarry Street. On the left is Guildford's oldest church, St Mary's, which is partly Saxon and is sometimes open to the public. On the right is the museum, and beyond a stone arch leading into the castle grounds. Turn left along Quarry Street and return to the bustling pedestrianised High Street with its cobbled surface. On Saturdays it is a Mecca for buskers and other street entertainers.

Once there were many coaching inns in the High Street, but of these the Angel Hotel is the only survivor. Looking up the road, one sees the Guildhall with its distinctive clock, with the Tunsgate – a covered area once used as a market – opposite. Beyond, the road leads to the Castle where little of historic interest remains, except for the walls of the keep, part of the dry moat, and some fragments of masonry. The grounds, to which admission is free, are owned by the borough, and are laid out as a garden with flower-beds, and winding paths offering views of the picturesque valley.

Returning once again to the High Street, Guildford House (a seventeenth-century town house) is on the left. This is also owned by the borough and used for art exhibitions, often with free admission. Just before the traffic lights, where North Street and Chertsey Street meet, Holy Trinity Church, a Victorian brick building, stands high on the right. The imposing Tudor brick building opposite – Abbot's Hospital – is an almshouse founded by George Abbot, a local worthy who became Archbishop of Canterbury. Beyond the traffic lights on the right is the Edward VI Grammar School with its chained library, while opposite is its more modern counterpart.

At the top of the High Street the road forks, the right turn leading to Clandon and Horsley, while on the left is London Road, wherein is situated the Civic Hall – used for concerts and functions. The Tourist Information Office (telephone 0483 575857) is also located here.

About 400 yards farther on is **London Road** Station – turn left at the traffic lights for the entrance, which is in York Road. You can either take a train from here, or return to the main station via High Street or North Street.

# 12

## LONDON WATERLOO–GUILDFORD– PORTSMOUTH HARBOUR
### by Ken Wright and Mark Hosking

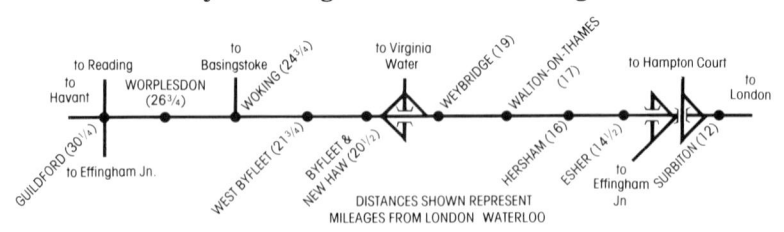

DISTANCES SHOWN REPRESENT MILEAGES FROM LONDON WATERLOO

The LSWR route to Portsmouth was a relatively late addition to the Victorian mainline railway network, not being completed until 1859, and the Harbour extension not until 1879.

**Waterloo** is the London terminus for the direct route to Portsmouth, as well as for services to Bournemouth and Salisbury. The present station, which was completed in 1922, offers the most pleasing impression of space and light. The designer, J. W. Jacomb-Hood, was much influenced by the station designs he had seen in the USA, and this is evident at Waterloo. The concourse is now much brighter and more cheerful than in bygone years, with a new tiled surface and a vast array of shops and restaurants, as well as a large travel centre and modern booking-office.

There are three trains an hour from Waterloo to Portsmouth – fast, semi-fast, and stopping. The fast and semi-fast trains usually depart from the middle number platforms in the centre of the concourse and the fast service normally includes a buffet car serving hot snacks.

Connections between the fast and stopping services are normally provided at Guildford. The best scenery on the line lies between Guildford and Havant, since the line has to traverse both the North and South Downs between these two points.

The journey out of Waterloo is on a viaduct all the way to **Clapham Junction**, which permits an elevated view of a large slice of the Inner South London suburbs. By sitting on the right-hand side of the carriage you will get a few glimpses of the newly cleaned Houses of Parliament and the large back garden of Lambeth Palace, the official residence of the Archbishop of Canterbury.

Through the gaps in the riverside office blocks next appears Vauxhall Bridge – worth a second glance for the carved statuettes, representing various deities, above the piers. At this point can be seen on the opposite bank of the Thames, the classical entrance and dome of the Tate Gallery, now the permanent home of the magnificent Joseph Turner Bequest.

After passing through **Vauxhall** Station which has recently seen major improvements, we pass by the New Covent Garden Market, formerly the site of Nine Elms Locomotive depot. It is a tragedy that the new market was not rail served, particularly as much produce originates from points south and west of the capital, including the Channel Islands. Do not miss at this point, on the opposite side, the famous landmark of Battersea power-station, alas no longer in active service, but about to rise from the ashes as a leisure centre.

Between **Queenstown Road** and **Clapham Junction** we pass through one of the busiest sections of track in the world. If anything resembles 'Spaghetti Junction' on the railway network then this is it. Clapham Junction itself is essentially three stations in one with the low-number Windsor line and Kensington Olympia platforms on the northern flank, the mainline and all other Waterloo services in the middle, and the high-number platforms for Victoria mainline and suburban services to the south. Any glance at a good railway map will show the reader how much of a fulcrum the station is for the south and south-west, and there are also a limited number of InterCity services to the Midlands and the North via Olympia.

Leaving Clapham Junction we speed onward through **Earlsfield** and after crossing the River Wandle we pass through **Wimbledon**. On your right you will notice the terminating platforms used by Underground District Line trains. After Wimbledon it can be truly said that we are now in the outer suburbs and the increasing amount of greenery from playing-fields, parks, and more spacious back gardens bears witness to this fact. We hurtle onwards past **Raynes Park** with its split platforms, the junction for Epsom and Chessington services; **New Malden** where Shepperton trains branch off; and **Berrylands** and **Surbiton**.

Surbiton is the junction for the secondary and more scenic route to Guildford via Cobham (described in Chapter 11) as well as for the Hampton Court branch. This junction is yet another of the 'flying' variety, much favoured by the LSWR, built to ensure a minimum of conflicting train movements, and thus speedier journeys.

We now pass through **Esher**, with the famous Sandown Racecourse clearly visible on our left, and then after crossing the River Mole, speed through **Hersham** and

57

**Walton-on-Thames**, among the increasing flora of the Thames Valley. After passing through **Weybridge**, the junction for Staines, we cross the River Wey and on our left between the trees can be seen the remains of a steep-banked corner of the former Brooklands race-track. Brooklands was dismantled at the start of hostilities in the Second World War as it would have served as a marker for German bombers for the adjacent aircraft works.

After **Byfleet** and **West Byfleet** which are effectively a continuation of Woking, we approach **Woking** itself. Look out for the distinctive Islamic architecture of the Woking Mosque on your left before entering the station. Woking is the point where the line to Portsmouth diverges from the mainline to Bournemouth and Salisbury. All scheduled Portsmouth services stop at Woking before veering south to Guildford. Local buses stop at Woking Station forecourt serving areas such as Knaphill, Bagshot, and Horsell.

Between Woking and Guildford there is one minor station, **Worplesdon**. We are now in Surrey heathland interspersed with small thickets, and pheasants with their splendid plumage are common along this section of track. As you approach **Guildford** keep an eye out for the imposing modern Anglican Cathedral on your right as you approach the station.

Guildford Station is at present a ramshackle affair – peeling paint, sagging roofs, and a general air of desolation confront the traveller entering Surrey's county town. However, work has recently begun on demolition of part of the present buildings, prior to commencement of major reconstruction of this once-impressive station (directions to the town centre and information about the town are contained in Chapter 11).

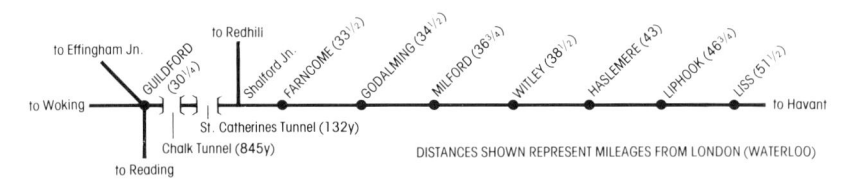

to Effingham Jn. — to Redhill — GUILDFORD (30¼) — Shalford Jn. — FARNCOME (33½) — GODALMING (34½) — MILFORD (36½) — WITLEY (38½) — HASLEMERE (43) — LIPHOOK (46½) — LISS (51½) — to Havant
to Woking
St. Catherines Tunnel (132y)
Chalk Tunnel (845y)
to Reading
DISTANCES SHOWN REPRESENT MILEAGES FROM LONDON (WATERLOO)

Immediately to the south of the station is the point at which the direct Portsmouth line bisects the North Downs, causing the route to go through two short tunnels. Shortly after leaving the second tunnel the line to Dorking and Redhill diverges to the left, and we follow the Wey Valley through **Farncombe** to **Godalming**. Godalming Station was recently refurbished with the help of the sponsorship of a local brewery, as can be seen from the station signs.

After leaving Godalming the Wey Valley quickly recedes behind us. We now commence the long climb to Haslemere through the Wealden country to one of the highest points on Network South East, via **Milford** and **Witley**. Between Witley and Haslemere the landscape is densely wooded and in autumn there is a vast splash of colour from the mix of conifers and deciduous woodland.

All scheduled services stop at **Haslemere**, which is situated in one of the most beautiful parts of the Surrey countryside. The town is known for its late summer Music Festival, now well established, in addition to its outstanding natural surroundings.

From the station it is a pleasant, and not too demanding, walk up to Gibbett Hill and the Devil's Punch Bowl. Turn right out of the station, under the bridge and continue until you reach a triangular green on your right. Turn right at the green, past a church, and continue on a minor road which eventually becomes a footpath and leads out to Gibbett Hill.

Gibbett Hill, so named because it was the local place of execution, is an outstanding viewpoint which overlooks the Devil's Punch Bowl. The latter is a particularly popular spot for walks, being situated next to the village of Hindhead with the main A3 road skirting its edge.

Back at Haslemere Station it is possible to take buses to areas such as Fernhurst, Henley, and Hindhead, although services have been subject to alteration since deregulation. The principal operator is Alder Valley and by using their services it is possible to make a visit to Petworth.

From the station, take a No. 229 bus to Midhurst, where you should change to a No. 225 to reach Petworth (at the time of writing the last bus back to Haslemere is at 5.50 p.m.). Petworth Park, immediately to the north and west of the town centre, is well worth visiting for its beautiful landscaped gardens designed by Capability Brown and its large house, both open to the public. The park contains a herd of deer and large man-made lake, views of which can be seen inside the house on canvases painted by Turner, who was a frequent visitor here after the death of his father in 1829.

After leaving the vicinity of Haslemere, the line descends towards **Liphook**, where on the right you can see a rail-served military depot. Shortly before entering **Liss** we cross the border into Hampshire. There used to be a line here coming from the right that went via Liss Forest to Bentley on the line to Alton, but it was closed during the Beeching era.

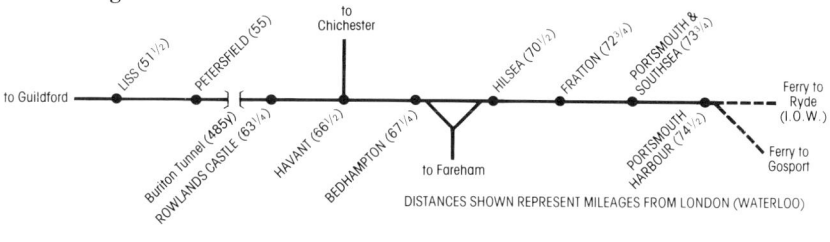

*[Route diagram: to Guildford — LISS (51½) — PETERSFIELD (55) — Buriton Tunnel (485y) — ROWLANDS CASTLE (63¼) — HAVANT (66½) — BEDHAMPTON (67¼) — to Chichester — HILSEA (70½) — FRATTON (72½) — PORTSMOUTH & SOUTHSEA (73½) — PORTSMOUTH HARBOUR (74½) — to Fareham — Ferry to Ryde (I.O.W.) — Ferry to Gosport. DISTANCES SHOWN REPRESENT MILEAGES FROM LONDON (WATERLOO)]*

The route now follows briefly the course of the River Rother until just before entering **Petersfield**. Until recently fast services did not stop here. Down services used to attain very high speeds at this point in the days of steam, right up until 1937 when the whole route was electrified.

Petersfield is a rather pleasant Hampshire market town, although on the debit side the main A3 Portsmouth Road runs through it. However, the traveller may care to pause to see the rather odd statue of William III (William of Orange), dressed in attire which resembles an outfit of the Roman period rather than the late seventeenth century. During the latter period, Samuel Pepys used to stop over at Petersfield on his way to Portsmouth, and he and his contemporaries had a penchant for living the good life while in the area.

It is possible to catch a bus from Petersfield to Selborne, well worth the trip since it was once the home of the renowned naturalist, Gilbert White. White wrote his celebrated book *The Natural History and Antiquities of Selborne* here in 1789. His former residence, The Wakes, is now a memorial library as well as being a museum dedicated to both White and Captain Oates of Antarctic fame.

After leaving Petersfield, the line goes under the main A3 road past some thickly wooded terrain on your right-hand side, with the northern side of the South Downs now looming into view. Near here is the viewpoint of Butser Hill, one of the highest points on the Downs. At this point we plunge through the short Buriton Tunnel, only 485 yards long, before emerging into a fold in the Downs with the steeper ground to the right.

By the time we come to the small (stopping services only) station at **Rowlands Castle** the hills are disappearing from view behind us and we approach the coastal plain on a right-hand curve. The former LBSCR line to Portsmouth comes in from your left just before reaching **Havant** Station. This junction was the scene of the infamous 'Battle of Havant', where navvies from both the South Western and Brighton companies armed with their tools, staged a pitched battle after the LBSCR padlocked a locomotive to the points in an attempt to stop the LSWR reaching Havant.

Havant has become something of an industrial sprawl on both sides of the track, but at least it is a sign that there has been a recent upturn in the local economy. The station, rebuilt just after the last war, was until 1963, the junction for Hayling Island. The island still attracts many visitors to its beaches and holiday camps – a regular bus service operated by Southdown leaves from the station forecourt. For further details of Hayling Island see Chapter 9.

About a mile farther on lies **Bedhampton**, which serves one of Havant's sprawling estates. From Bedhampton the line curves gently towards Portsmouth, cutting under the A3 Motorway and bringing Portsea Downs into view to the north, their suburban slopes contrasting with the woods and meadows of their Sussex counterparts. To the south, obscured by the A27 coast road, lie the marshes of Langstone Harbour. Protected from man by the barriers of road and rail, these wetlands are rich in bird life, the most satisfying access being by dinghy from Hayling Island, or, for landlubbers, a careful walk from Eastney on Portsea Island itself.

At Farlington's triangular junction, the line ahead stretches away towards Fareham, Eastleigh, and Southampton, while the Portsmouth line swings south, dives under the A27, and prepares to broach this great city's outer defences. The first of these is Portsea Creek, the narrow waterway which creates Portsea Island, while the second is a huge wall-topped mound through which the railway cuts to re-emerge on the old airfield, now smothered in hi-tech factories, warehouses, and a somewhat incongruous golf-course, all served by **Hilsea**.

Heading southwards now, the line bisects the Island, through rows of terraced houses, once the home of thousands of civilian dockyard workers, to reach the huge railway yards at **Fratton**. Set in a triangle amid the mainline, the long-disused branch to Southsea, and Fratton Park (ancestral home of Portsmouth Town Football Club), the yards – which once continually resounded to a symphony for steam-whistle and clanging buffers – are now home only to lines of facelessly efficient EMUs, the civil servants of the railway world.

Curving through the station to regain its westerly course, the line enters a wide cutting, once a canal, for the run into the heart of the town. **Portsmouth and Southsea** Station was the original terminus of the line, lying on the edge of the Royal Dockyards inner defences. Indeed its original and still locally used name of Portsmouth Town indicates its proximity to the city centre, with the modern shopping centre, Guildhall, and County cricket ground all located near by.

For a town of comparable size to Brighton, the present station is disappointing to say the least. Some of the low-level terminal platforms are now disused, since the bulk of services now run up the steep ramp to the high level and continue on to the harbour. However, plans for the rebuilding of the high-level station have recently been announced, and the work was due to take place in February/March 1988.

At the end of the high-level platform, the course of the Dock branch can be seen curving away to the right, while the mainline curves left on a high embankment past the cricket ground. In case you were in any doubt that Portsmouth was a naval stronghold, you now have proof galore. On your left after crossing the main road, you have the United Services Portsmouth sports ground, before the cranes and superstructure of the dockyards loom on the horizon. After swinging to the right and then left, we enter **Portsmouth Harbour** Station.

The Harbour Station is built on its own pier, the seaward end of which is used as a terminal for ferries to the Isle of Wight, and Gosport – just across the harbour.

You literally walk off the train across the short concourse and down the gangway ahead for the ferry to Ryde Pier Head or bear right for the Gosport ferry. The Isle of Wight service was formerly part of BR, but even under privately owned Sealink, the ferries, which are modern catamarans, remain integrated with the fast trains to and from London.

From the station forecourt it is possible to catch buses to many local destinations such as Waterlooville and Hambleton, the main operator here being Southdown. The bus station, known as the 'Hard Interchange', also houses the Tourist Information Centre (telephone 0705 826722/3) which is open all year. The main public entrance to the docks, where continental car ferries now share the facilities, is across the Hard to the left.

# THE CITY OF PORTSMOUTH
## by Ken Wright

The City of Portsmouth was initially granted its Town Charter in 1194 by Richard I, although the northern edge of the harbour had been used by the Romans – it was there that they constructed Portchester Castle. Portsmouth Cathedral was founded in 1185.

In the fifteenth century the way was paved for making Portsmouth the bustling place it is today, with the construction of the dry dock, ramparts, and other defence works. From this time on the town became of increasing importance to the Navy. It remains a naval base today, housing all types of naval vessels including submarines. The ferry terminals at Portsmouth Harbour and Gosport make excellent vantage points, and at certain times it is also possible to make a motor launch trip round the harbour.

On certain days of the year, particularly in August, parts of the Royal Naval Dockyard are thrown open to the public. Throughout the year, in the Naval Heritage Area, three minutes' walk from the Harbour Station, you can go on board HMS *Victory*, Nelson's famous flagship, and view the conservation taking place on Henry VIII's *Mary Rose*. You can also explore Britain's first battleship HMS *Warrior*, recently returned to Portsmouth for preservation, and visit the Royal Naval Museum.

Offshore in the Solent, several naval batteries and forts can be clearly seen. These were constructed mostly between 1850 and 1860 by the then Prime Minister, Lord Palmerston, who also ordered work to commence on fortifications on top of Portsdown Hill, overlooking the city. Because of its naval connections, Portsmouth became a prime target in the last war and Pompey took a hammering. The area near the modern city centre was particularly badly hit, including the imposing Guildhall, which was reconstructed out of the shell that remained after hostilities ceased. Today the whole of Portsea Island is built up and even stretches on to the mainland in the north. The development area around Portsmouth includes both Gosport and Portchester.

Gosport (God's Port) founded by Henry de Blois in 1158 is possibly an even better place than Portsmouth to view the harbour. Near to HMS *Dolphin*, the training station for crews on submarines, is the Royal Naval Submarine Museum. Exhibits include the historic *Holland I*, which inadvertently sank in 1913 after being towed away for cutting.

Portchester is famous for its castle, which was constructed in typical Roman fashion about the third century AD. Its walls are approximately 10 feet thick by 20 feet high and provide some of the finest Roman remains in northern Europe. It appears to have been occupied at some stage in the Saxon era, and a castle keep and moat were added in the twelfth century. Portchester can be reached either by local trains to **Portchester** Station or by Southdown buses No. 347 or No. 716.

# FURTHER INFORMATION

**Places to Visit**
Unless otherwise indicated, there is an admission charge payable for museums, castles, historic houses, etc., described in the text. A very useful booklet *Hundreds of Places to Visit in South-East England* is published by the South-East England Tourist Board, 1 Warwick Park, Tunbridge Wells, Kent TN2 5TA, price £1 (in 1987).

The National Trust produces a free leaflet giving brief details of properties open in Surrey, Sussex, Hampshire, and the Isle of Wight. The Southern Regional Office at Polesden Lacey (telephone Bookham 53401) will assist with general enquiries about admission to Trust properties in the area.

The Redundant Churches Fund, St Andrew-by-the-Wardrobe, Queen Victoria Street, London EC4 5DE, telephone 01–248 7461, can provide details of opening arrangements and other information in respect of churches in their care.

**Maps**
The Editor recommends:
 (1) Ordnance Survey 'Routemaster' 1:250,000 series Map 9 for route-planning, by train or otherwise, in the whole of South-East England;
 (2) Ordnance Survey 'Landranger' 1:50,000 series for local route-finding and country walking;
 (3) Ordnance Survey 'Pathfinder' 1:25,000 series for finding your way around a particular village – especially useful for ramblers as it shows the precise position of footpaths (in relation to field boundaries, etc.);
 (4) Estate Publications, Bridewell House, Tenterden, Kent, for attractive two-colour town-plan booklets; there is a separate booklet for each conurbation together with its outlying villages, and there are separate Surrey and Sussex booklets giving just town-centre maps for the whole county.

These are all available from good bookshops, although specific towns are generally only available locally.

**Timetables**
(1) British Rail sells a passenger timetable for the whole country (of some 1,400 pages) which it publishes twice a year, in mid May and early October. It is available both at stations and bookshops, and can usually be consulted in public libraries. BR also gives away free pocket timetables and leaflets, and sells local derivative timetable booklets covering groups of train services (Booklets F, G, and J cover the routes in this guide-book).

(2) Bus companies generally publish free timetable leaflets for related groups of routes, but sometimes a booklet for a whole conurbation. These are generally only available from company offices in town centres in shopping hours (not always on Saturday afternoon), from village bus information points, or by post from the company. Bus timetables are liable to change at unspecified dates and are often not displayed at bus stops because of vandalism.

**Principal Bus Operators**
Alder Valley, Halimote Road, Aldershot GU11 3EG (telephone Aldershot 27181).
 Hastings & District Transport Ltd, Beaufort Road, Silverhill, St Leonards-on-Sea, East Sussex (telephone Hastings (0424) 433711).
 London Country South-West, Lesbourne Road, Reigate, Surrey RH2 7LE (telephone Reigate 242411).
 Maidstone & District Motor Services Ltd, Luton Road, Chatham ME5 7LH (telephone 0634 47334).
 Southdown Motor Services Ltd, Walmers Lane, School Hill, Lewes, East Sussex (telephone Brighton 480248).
 Tillingbourne Bus Co. Ltd, Little Mead, Cranleigh, nr Guildford, Surrey (telephone 0483 276880).
 In addition, Surrey County Council produces a series of six timetable booklets covering the county – details from the Transportation Planning Unit, County Hall, Kingston upon Thames, KT1 2DN (telephone 01–541 9371); and East Sussex County Council publishes the free *Bus Guide: map and list of bus/rail services in East Sussex*, available from the County Engineer, Phoenix Causeway, Lewes, East Sussex BN7 1UE (telephone 0273-475400).

# THE RAILWAY DEVELOPMENT SOCIETY

**The Railway Development Society (RDS)** is a national, voluntary, independent body which campaigns for better rail services, for both passengers and freight, and greater use of public transport.

It publishes books and papers, holds meetings and exhibitions, runs special trains, and generally endeavours to put the case for rail to politicians, civil servants, commerce and industry, and the public at large; as well as feeding users' comments and suggestions to British Rail management and unions. The Society also gives help to local user groups and provides a forum for the exchange of ideas between both groups and individuals.

RDS has fifteen branches. The London and Home Counties Branch covers a wide area around London, including the area covered by this book, except for some parts of West Sussex which belong to the Wessex Branch.

Membership is open to all who are in general agreement with the aims of the Society; subscriptions (1988) are: standard £7.50; reduced rate (for pensioners, full-time students, and unemployed people) £4; families £7.50 plus £1 per household member.

For more details, write either to the Membership Promotion Officer, Mr L. J. Boylett, 15 Athenaeum Road, Whetstone, London N20 9AA or else to the Membership Secretary, Mr F. J. Hastilow, 49 Irnham Road, Four Oaks, Sutton Coldfield, West Midlands B74 2TQ.

# LOCAL RAIL USER GROUPS

East Sussex Travellers' Association: Covers stations Eridge to Uckfield, and the Tunbridge Wells–Groombridge rail-replacement bus, and local buses. Secretary: Mrs G. I. Gow, 36 Framfield Road, Uckfield, East Sussex.

Dorking and District Rail Users' Association: Barry Collins, Sunridge, South Drive, Dorking, Surrey RH5 4AG.

Edenbridge and District Rail Travellers' Association: Covers stations Edenbridge (Redhill–Tonbridge line) and Edenbridge Town–Ashurst (Uckfield line). Secretary: Mr J. A. Bigny, 15 Plough Walk, Edenbridge, Kent TN8 6DU.

National Federation of Bus Users: Secretary: Michael Dearing, 6 Holmhurst Lane, St Leonards-on-Sea, East Sussex TN37 7LW.

Reigate, Redhill and District Railways Users' Association: RDS Representative: Andrew Harris, 25 Palmer Close, Redhill, Surrey RH1 4BU.

Transport Users' Group of Hastings, Bexhill and District: Covers stations in Hastings, Bexhill, Battle, and Rye areas and local buses. Secretary/Treasurer: Michael Dearing, 6 Holmhurst Lane, St Leonards-on-Sea, East Sussex TN37 7LW.

# SELECT BIBLIOGRAPHY

Armstrong, J. R., *A History of Sussex* (Darwen Finlayson Ltd, 1961).
Brandon, P., *The Sussex Landscape* (Hodder and Stoughton, 1974).
Cooper, B. K., *Rail Centres: Brighton* (Ian Allan, 1981).
Course, E., *The Railways of Southern England* (Batsford).
Davies, R. and Grant, M., *London and its Railways* (David & Charles).
Glover, G., *Britain's Local Railways – Southern England* (Ian Allan, 1983).
Goldring, P., *Britain by Train* (Ian Allan).
Gray, A., *The London to Brighton Line* (Oakwood Press, 1977).
Hadfield, J. (ed.), *The Shell Guide to England* (Book Club, 1973).
Hodd, H. R., *The Horsham–Guildford Direct Railway* (Oakwood Press, 1975).
Jackson, A., *London's Termini* (David & Charles).
Marsden, C., *Southern Rails in the 1980s* (Ian Allan).
Mitchell, V. and Smith, K., *South Coast Railways – Worthing to Chichester* (Middleton Press, 1983).
Mitchell, V. and Smith, K., *Southern Main Lines – Crawley to Littlehampton* (Middleton Press, 1986).

Moody, G. T., *Southern Electric 1909–1979* (Ian Allan, 5th edition, 1979).
White, H. P., *A Regional History of the Railways of Great Britain – Volume 2: Southern England* (David & Charles, 1961).
*AA Illustrated Guide to Britain's Coast* (Drive Publications).
*AA Book of British Villages* (Drive Publications).
*Hundreds of Places to Visit in South East England* (South East England Tourist Board).
*Modern Railways* (various issues).
*Railway Magazine* (various issues).
*Railways South East* (Winter 1987–88).

We should like to express our particular thanks to the staff at Brixton Reference Library and the Harvard Reference Library (Southwark) for being so helpful in searching for material.

# INDEX

Amberley 38–39
Angmering 42
Arundel 39, 40
Ashtead 33
Ashurst 18

Balcombe 10
Barnham 39, 42–43
Beachy Head 28, 30
Betchworth 50
Bexhill 31
Bignor Roman Villa 38
Billingshurst 37–38
Bluebell Railway 15–16
Bognor Regis 39
Bookham 54
Bosham 44–45
Boxhill & Westhumble 34
Brighton 11–12
Burgess Hill 10
Buxted 20

Chalk Pits Museum 39
Cheam 33
Chichester 43–44, 46–47
Chilworth 48–49
Christ's Hospital 37
Clandon 53
Claygate 52
Cobham & Stoke D'Abernon 52
Cooden Beach 31
Cowden 18
Crawley 10, 37
Crowborough & Jarvis Brook 20
Croydon 8, 12–13

Devil's Dyke 10, 12
Devil's Punch Bowl 58–59
Ditchling Beacon 25
Dorking 34–35, 50
Dorking (Deepdene) 50
Dorking West 49–50
Dormans 15

Eastbourne 28, 29–30
East Grinstead 15
Edenbridge 24
Edenbridge Town 17–18
Effingham Junction 53, 54
Emsworth 45
Epsom 33

Eridge 19–20
Esher 57
Ewell 33

Falmer 29
Faygate 37
Ferring 42
Fishbourne 44
Ford 39
Fratton 60

Gatwick Airport 9
Glynde 29
Godalming 58
Godstone 24
Gomshall 49
Goring-by-Sea 42
Gosport 60, 61
Guildford 47, 48, 53–56, 58

Hampden Park 29
Haslemere 58–59
Hassocks 10
Hastings 32
Havant 45, 60
Hayling Island 45
Haywards Heath 10
Hever 18
Holmwood 35
Horsham 36, 37
Horsley 53
Hove 41
Hurst Green 14, 17

Ifield 37

Lancing 42
Lavender Line 21
Leatherhead 33, 54
Leigh 23
Leith Hill 49
Lewes 25–26
Lingfield 14–15
Littlehampton 39
Littlehaven 37

Midhurst 43, 47, 59

Newhaven 26–27
Normans Bay 31
Nutfield 24

Ockley 35–36
Oxshott 52
Oxted 14, 16–17

Pagham 43
Penshurst 23
Petersfield 59
Petworth 59
Pevensey 30-31
Plumpton 25
Polegate 29
Portsmouth 60–61
Pulborough 38

Redhill 8
Reigate 50–51

St Leonards 32
Seaford 27
Selsey Bill 43
Seven Sisters 27–28
Shalford 48
Shere 49
Shoreham-by-Sea 41
Singleton 47
Southease 26
Surbiton 51
Sutton 32–33

Three Bridges 10
Tonbridge 22–23
Tunbridge Wells & Eridge Railway Preservation Society 19

Uckfield 20–21

Volks Electric Railway 11

Warnham 36
Weald and Downland Open Air Museum 47
West Dean 47
Wildfowl Trust 40
Wimbledon 57
Woking 58
Woldingham 13
Worthing 42

ISBN 0-7117-0331-0
© 1988 Railway Development Society
Printed and published in Great Britain by Jarrold and Sons Ltd, Norwich. 1/88